OUTLINES
OF
PYRRHONISM

Translated by
R. G. Bury

SEXTUS
EMPIRICUS

GREAT BOOKS IN PHILOSOPHY

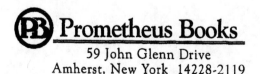
Prometheus Books

59 John Glenn Drive
Amherst, New York 14228-2119

Published 1990 by Prometheus Books

59 John Glenn Drive
Amherst, New York 14228-2119
VOICE: 716-691-0133, ext.210
FAX: 716-691-0137
WWW.PROMETHEUSBOOKS.COM

Library of Congress Catalog Number: 89-64198

ISBN 13: 978-0-87975-597-3

ISBN 10: 0-87975-597-0

OUTLINES
OF
PYRRHONISM

Great Books in Philosophy Series
(Metaphysics/Epistemology)

See the back of this volume for a complete list of titles in Prometheus's Great Books in Philosophy and Great Minds series.

SEXTUS EMPIRICUS, physician and philosopher, wrote in the latter part of the third century A.D. Little is known of Sextus' life. He seems to have resided for a while in Rome and later in Alexandria.

Though his medical writings are lost, Sextus' surviving philosophical works are *Outlines of Pyrrhonism, Against the Dogmatists, Against the Logicians, Against the Physicists, Against the Ethicists,* and *Against the Professors.* Also ascribed to him are a treatise *On the Soul* and *Notes on Medicine.*

Sextus represented the new skeptical school founded by Aenesidemus of Cnossos, whose system Sextus endeavored to clarify. Briefly, the skeptics devoted themselves to critiquing and pointing out the shortcomings of every positive philosophical doctrine. Sextus himself was a major proponent of the Pyrrhonistic "suspension of judgment" (named for the philosopher Pyrrho of Elis [ca. 360–270 B.C.]), which maintained that we can obtain no undeniably true knowledge of reality. This being the case, we should refrain from forming judgments about things we cannot truly understand.

While Sextus' writings may appear wanting in originality, they are a valuable compilation of the work of his predecessors, and for this very reason, they provide us with a much needed description of ancient skepticism.

CONTENTS

BOOK I

CONTENTS

CONTENTS

BOOK II

CONTENTS

CONTENTS

OUTLINES OF PYRRHONISM

BOOK I

CHAPTER I. OF THE MAIN DIFFERENCE BETWEEN PHILOSOPHIC SYSTEMS

The natural result of any investigation is that the **1** investigators either discover the object of search or deny that it is discoverable and confess it to be inapprehensible or persist in their search. So, too, with **2** regard to the objects investigated by philosophy, this is probably why some have claimed to have discovered the truth, others have asserted that it cannot be apprehended, while others again go on inquiring. Those who believe they have discovered it are the "dog- **3** matists," specially so called—Aristotle, for example, and Epicurus* and the Stoics† and certain others; Cleitomachus and Carneades and other Academics‡

---

*[341-270 B.C. Epicurus argued that our senses come into direct contact with objects via "effluences" that emanate from the objects themselves.]

†[For the Stoics, virtue was based on true knowledge and the knowledge of the wise man consisted in the agreement of his mental conceptions with reality. These conceptions corresponded exactly to real things, and could not have been produced by other causes.]

[‡The Academics, exemplified by Arcesilaus (ca. 315-240 B.C.), founder of the middle Academy, denied the accuracy of any knowledge, particularly any putative knowledge derived from sense perception.]

4 treat it as inapprehensible: the skeptics keep on searching. Hence it seems reasonable to hold that the main types of philosophy are three—the dogmatic, the Academic, and the skeptic. Of the other systems it will best become others to speak: our task at present is to describe in outline the skeptic doctrine, first premising that of none of our future statements do we positively affirm that the fact is exactly as we state it, but we simply record each fact, like a chronicler, as it appears to us at the moment.

CHAPTER II. OF THE ARGUMENTS OF SKEPTICISM

5 Of the skeptic philosophy one argument (or branch of exposition) is called "general," the other "special." In the general argument we set forth the distinctive features of skepticism, stating its purport and principles, its logical methods, criterion, and end or aim; the "tropes," also, or "modes," which lead to suspension of judgment, and in what sense we adopt the skeptic formulae, and the distinction between skepticism and the philosophies which stand next to **6** it. In the special argument we state our objections regarding the several divisions of so-called philosophy. Let us, then, deal first with the general argument, beginning our description with the names given to the skeptic school.

Chapter III. Of the Nomenclature of Skepticism

The skeptic school, then, is also called "zetetic" from **7** its activity in investigation and inquiry, and "ephetic" or suspensive from the state of mind produced in the inquirer after his search, and "aporetic" or dubitative either from its habit of doubting and seeking, as some say, or from its indecision as regards assent and denial, and "Pyrrhonean" from the fact that Pyrrho appears to us to have applied himself to skepticism more thoroughly and more conspicuously than his predecessors.

Chapter IV. What Skepticism is

Skepticism is an ability, or mental attitude, which **8** opposes appearances to judgments in any way whatsoever, with the result that, owing to the equipollence of the objects and reasons thus opposed, we are brought firstly to a state of mental suspense and next to a state of "unperturbedness" or quietude. Now we call it an "ability" not in any subtle sense, but **9** simply in respect of its "being able." By "appearances" we now mean the objects of sense perception, whence we contrast them with the objects of thought or "judgments." The phrase "in any way whatsoever" can be connected either with the word "ability," to make us take the word "ability," as we said, in its simple sense, or with the phrase "opposing appearances to judgments"; for inasmuch as we oppose these in a variety of ways—appearances to appearances, or judgments to judgments, or *alternando* appearances to judgments,—in order to ensure the inclusion of all these antitheses we employ the phrase "in any way whatsoever." Or, again, we join "in any way whatsoever" to "appearances and judgments" in order that we may not have to inquire how the appearances appear or how the thought objects are judged, but **10** may take these terms in the simple sense. The phrase "opposed judgments" we do not employ in the sense of negations and affirmations only but simply as equivalent to "conflicting judgments." "Equipollence" we use of equality in respect of probability and improbability, to indicate that no one of the conflicting judgments takes precedence of any other as being more probable. "Suspense" is a state of mental rest owing to which we neither deny nor affirm anything. "Quietude" is an untroubled and tranquil condition of soul. And how quietude enters the soul along with suspension of judgment we shall explain in our chapter (XII) "Concerning the End."

CHAPTER V. OF THE SKEPTIC

11 In the definition of the skeptic system there is also implicitly included that of the Pyrrhonean philosopher: he is the man who participates in this "ability."

CHAPTER VI. OF THE PRINCIPLES OF SKEPTICISM

12 The originating cause of skepticism is, we say, the hope of attaining quietude. Men of talent, who were perturbed by the contradictions in things and in doubt as to which of the alternatives they ought to accept, were led on to inquire what is true in things and what false, hoping by the settlement of this question to attain quietude. The main basic principle of the skeptic system is that of opposing to every proposition an equal proposition; for we believe that as a consequence of this we end by ceasing to dogmatize.

CHAPTER VII. DOES THE SKEPTIC DOGMATIZE?

When we say that the skeptic refrains from dog- **13** matizing we do not use the term "dogma," as some do, in the broader sense of "approval of a thing" (for the skeptic gives assent to the feelings which are the necessary results of sense impressions, and he would not, for example, say when feeling hot or cold "I believe that I am not hot or cold"); but we say that "he does not dogmatize," using "dogma" in the sense, which some give it, of "assent to one of the nonevident objects of scientific inquiry"; for the Pyrrhonean philosopher assents to nothing that is nonevident. Moreover, even in the act of enunciating **14** the skeptic formulae concerning things nonevident— such as the formula "No more (one thing or another)," or the formula "I determine nothing," or any of the others which we shall presently mention,—he does not dogmatize. For whereas the dogmatizer posits the things about which he is said to be dogmatizing as really existent, the skeptic does not posit these formulae in any absolute sense; for he conceives that, just as the formula "All things are false" asserts the falsity of itself as well as of everything else, as does the formula "Nothing is true," so also the formula "No more" asserts that itself, like all the rest, is "No more (this than that)," and thus cancels itself along with the rest. And of the other formulae we say the **15** same. If then, while the dogmatizer posits the matter of his dogma as substantial truth, the skeptic enunciates his formulae so that they are virtually cancelled by themselves, he should not be said to dogmatize in his enunciation of them. And, most important of all, in his enunciation of these formulae he states what appears to himself and announces his own impression in an undogmatic way, without making any positive assertion regarding the external realities.

Chapter VIII. Has the Skeptic a Doctrinal Rule?

16 We follow the same lines in replying to the question "Has the skeptic a doctrinal rule?" For if one defines a "doctrinal rule" as "adherence to a number of dogmas which are dependent both on one another and on appearances," and defines "dogma" as "assent to a nonevident proposition," then we shall say that he **17** has not a doctrinal rule. But if one defines "doctrinal rule" as "procedure which, in accordance with appearance, follows a certain line of reasoning, that reasoning indicating how it is possible to live rightly (the word 'rightly' being taken, not as referring to virtue only, but in a wider sense) and tending to enable one to suspend judgment," then we say that he has a doctrinal rule. For we follow a line of reasoning which, in accordance with appearances, points us to a life comfortable with the customs of our country and its laws and institutions, and to our own instinctive feelings.

CHAPTER IX. DOES THE SKEPTIC DEAL WITH PHYSICS?

We make a similar reply also to the question "Should **18** the skeptic deal with physical problems?" For while, on the one hand, so far as regards making firm and positive assertions about any of the matters dogmatically treated in physical theory, we do not deal with physics; yet, on the other hand, in respect of our mode of opposing to every proposition an equal proposition and of our theory of quietude, we do treat of physics. This, too, is the way in which we approach the logical and ethical branches of so-called "philosophy."

CHAPTER X. DO THE SKEPTICS ABOLISH APPEARANCES?

Those who say that "the skeptics abolish appearan- **19** ces," or phenomena, seem to me to be unacquainted with the statements of our school. For, as we said above, we do not overthrow the affective sense impressions which induce our assent involuntarily; and these impressions are "the appearances." And when we question whether the underlying object is such as it appears, we grant the fact that it appears, and

our doubt does not concern the appearance itself but the account given of that appearance,—and that is a different thing from questioning the appearance
20 itself. For example, honey appears to us to be sweet (and this we grant, for we perceive sweetness through the senses), but whether it is also sweet in its essence is for us a matter of doubt, since this is not an appearance but a judgment regarding the appearance. And even if we do actually argue against the appearances, we do not propound such arguments with the intention of abolishing appearances, but by way of pointing out the rashness of the dogmatists; for if reason is such a trickster as to all but snatch away the appearances from under our very eyes, surely we should view it with suspicion in the case of things nonevident so as not to display rashness by following it.

Chapter XI. Of the Criterion of Skepticism

21 That we adhere to appearances is plain from what we say about the criterion of the skeptic school. The word "criterion" is used in two senses: in the one it means "the standard regulating belief in reality or unreality," (and this we shall discuss in our refutation); in the other it denotes the standard of action by conforming to which in the conduct of life we perform some actions and abstain from others; and it is of
22 the latter that we are now speaking. The criterion, then, of the skeptic school is, we say, the appearance, giving this name to what is virtually the sense presen-

tation. For since this lies in feeling and involuntary affection, it is not open to question. Consequently, no one, I suppose, disputes that the underlying object has this or that appearance; the point in dispute is whether the object is in reality such as it appears to be.

Adhering, then, to appearances we live in ac- **23** cordance with the normal rules of life, undogmatically, seeing that we cannot remain wholly inactive. And it would seem that this regulation of life is fourfold, and that one part of it lies in the guidance of nature, another in the constraint of the passions, another in the tradition of laws and customs, another in the instruction of the arts. Nature's guidance is **24** that by which we are naturally capable of sensation and thought; constraint of the passions is that whereby hunger drives us to food and thirst to drink; tradition of customs and laws, that whereby we regard piety in the conduct of life as good, but impiety as evil; instruction of the arts, that whereby we are not inactive in such arts as we adopt. But we make all these statements undogmatically.

CHAPTER XII. WHAT IS THE END OF SKEPTICISM?

Our next subject will be the end of the skeptic system. **25** Now an "end" is "that for which all actions or reasonings are undertaken, while it exists for the sake of none"; or, otherwise, "the ultimate object of appentency." We assert still that the skeptic's end is quietude in respect of matters of opinion and moderate feeling

26 in respect of things unavoidable. For the skeptic, having set out to philosophize with the object of passing judgment on the sense impressions and ascertaining which of them are true and which false, so as to attain quietude thereby, found himself involved in contradictions of equal weight, and being unable to decide between them suspended judgment; and as he was thus in suspense there followed, as it happened, the state of quietude in respect of matters **27** of opinion. For the man who opines that anything is by nature good or bad is for ever being disquieted: when he is without the things which he deems good he believes himself to be tormented by things naturally bad and he pursues after the things which are, as he thinks, good; which when he has obtained he keeps falling into still more perturbations because of his irrational and immoderate elation, and in his dread of a change of fortune he uses every endeavor to avoid losing the things which he deems good. On **28** the other hand, the man who determines nothing as to what is naturally good or bad neither shuns nor pursues anything eagerly; and, in consequence, he is unperturbed.

The skeptic, in fact, had the same experience which is said to have befallen the painter Apelles.* Once, they say, when he was painting a horse and wished to represent in the painting the horse's foam, he was so unsuccessful that he gave up the attempt and flung at the picture the sponge on which he used

---

*Court painter to Alexander the Great (ca. 350–300 B.C.).

to wipe the paints off his brush, and the mark of the sponge produced the effect of a horse's foam. So, too, the skeptics were in hopes of gaining quietude **29** by means of a decision regarding the disparity of the objects of sense and of thought, and being unable to effect this they suspended judgment; and they found that quietude, as if by chance, followed upon their suspense, even as a shadow follows its substance. We do not, however, suppose that the skeptic is wholly untroubled; but we say that he is troubled by things unavoidable; for we grant that he is cold at times and thirsty, and suffers various affections of that kind. But even in these cases, whereas ordinary people are **30** afflicted by two circumstances,—namely, by the affections themselves and, in no less a degree, by the belief that these conditions are evil by nature,—the skeptic, by his rejection of the added belief in the natural badness of all these conditions, escapes here too with less discomfort. Hence we say that, while in regard to matters of opinion the skeptic's end is quietude, in regard to things unavoidable it is "moderate affection." But some notable skeptics have added the further definition "suspension of judgment in investigations."

CHAPTER XIII. OF THE GENERAL MODES LEADING TO SUSPENSION OF JUDGEMENT

Now that we have been saying that tranquillity follows **31** on suspension of judgment, it will be our next task to explain how we arrive at this suspension. Speaking generally, one may say that it is the result of setting things in opposition. We oppose either appearances to appearances or objects of thought to objects of **32** thought or *alternando*. For instance, we oppose appearances to appearances when we say "The same tower appears round from a distance, but square from close at hand"; and thoughts to thoughts, when in answer to him who argues the existence of providence from the order of the heavenly bodies we oppose the fact that often the good fare ill and the bad fare well, and draw from this the inference that providence **33** does not exist. And thoughts we oppose to appearances, as when Anaxagoras* countered the notion that snow is white with the argument, "Snow is frozen water, and water is black; therefore snow also is black." With a different idea we oppose things present sometimes to things present, as in the foregoing examples, and sometimes to things past or future, as, for instance, when someone propounds to us a theory **34** which we are unable to refute, we say to him in reply, "Just as, before the birth of the founder of the school to which you belong, the theory it holds was not as yet apparent as a sound theory, although it was really in existence, so likewise it is possible that the opposite theory to that which you now propound is already existent, though not yet apparent to us, so that we ought not as yet to yield assent to this theory which at the moment seems to be valid."

---

*[Ca. 500–428 B.C. He held that all natural objects are composed of minute particles containing mixtures of all qualities, and that mind or intelligence (*nous*) acts upon masses of these particles to create objects.]

But in order that we may have a more exact **35** understanding of these antitheses I will describe the modes by which suspension of judgment is brought about, but without making any positive assertion regarding either their number or their validity; for it is possible that they may be unsound or there may be more of them than I shall enumerate.

Chapter XIV. Concerning the Ten Modes

The usual tradition amongst the older skeptics is that **36** the "modes" by which "suspension" is supposed to be brought about are ten in number; and they also give them the synonymous names of "arguments" and "positions." They are these: the first, based on the variety in animals; the second, on the differences in human beings; the third, on the different structures of the organs of sense; the fourth, on the circum-stantial conditions; the fifth, on positions and intervals and locations; the sixth, on intermixtures; the seventh, **37** on the quantities and formations of the underlying objects; the eighth, on the fact of relativity; the ninth, on the frequency or rarity of occurrence; the tenth, on the disciplines and customs and laws, the legendary beliefs and the dogmatic convictions. This order, **38** however, we adopt without prejudice.

As superordinate to these there stand three modes—that based on the subject who judges, that on the object judged, and that based on both. The first four of the ten modes are subordinate to the mode based on the subject (for the subject which judges is either an animal or a man or a sense, and existent in some condition): the seventh and tenth modes are referred to that based on the object judged: the fifth, sixth, eighth, and ninth are referred to the **39** mode based on both subject and object. Furthermore, these three modes are also referred to that of relation, so that the mode of relation stands as the highest *genus,* and the three as *species,* and the ten as subordinate *subspecies.* We give this as the probable account of their numbers; and as to their argumentative force what we say is this:

40 The *first* argument (or *trope*), as we said, is that which shows that the same impressions are not produced by the same objects owing to the differences in animals. This we infer both from the differences in their origins and from the variety of their bodily **41** structures. Thus, as to origin, some animals are produced without sexual union, others by coition. And of those produced without coition, some come from fire, like the animalcules which appear in furnaces, others from putrid water, like gnats; others from wine when it turns sour, like ants; others from earth, like grasshoppers; others from marsh, like frogs; others from mud, like worms; others from asses, like beetles; others from greens, like caterpillars; others from fruits, like the gall insects in wild figs; others from rotting animals, as bees from bulls and wasps from **42** horses. Of the animals generated by coition, some— in fact the majority—come from homogeneous parents, others from heterogeneous parents, as do mules. Again, of animals in general, some are born alive, like men; others are born as eggs, like birds; and yet others as lumps of flesh, like bears. It is natural, then, that these dissimilar and variant modes **43** of birth should produce much contrariety of sense affection, and that this is a source of its divergent, discordant, and conflicting character.

Moreover, the differences found in the most im- **44** portant parts of the body, and especially in those of which the natural function is judging and per- ceiving, are capable of producing a vast deal of diver- gence in the sense impressions owing to the variety in the animals. Thus, sufferers from jaundice declare that objects which seem to us white are yellow, while those whose eyes are bloodshot call them blood-red. Since, then, some animals have eyes which are yellow, others bloodshot, others albino, others of other colors, they probably, I suppose, have different perceptions of color. Moreover, if we bend down over a book **45** after having gazed long and fixedly at the sun, the letters seem to us to be golden in color and circling round. Since, then, some animals possess also a natural brilliance in their eyes, and emit from them a fine and mobile stream of light, so that they can even see by night, we seem bound to suppose that they are differently affected from us by external objects. Jugglers, too, by means of smearing lamp- **46** wicks with the rust of copper or with the juice of the cuttlefish make the bystanders appear now cop- per-colored and now black—and that by just a small sprinkling of extra matter. Surely, then, we have much more reason to suppose that when different juices are intermingled in the vision of animals their impressions of the objects will become different. Again, 47 when we press the eyeball at one side the forms, figures, and sizes of the objects appear oblong and narrow. So it is probable that all animals which have the pupil of the eye slanting and elongated—such as goats, cats, and similar animals—have impressions of the objects which are different and unlike the notions formed of them by the animals which have 48 round pupils. Mirrors, too, owing to differences in their construction, represent the external objects at one time as very small—as when the mirror is concave,—at another time as elongated and narrow— as when the mirror is convex. Some mirrors, too, show the head of the figure reflected at the bottom 49 and the feet at the top. Since, then, some organs of sight actually protrude beyond the face owing to their convexity, while others are quite concave, and others again lie in a level plane, on this account also it is probable that their impressions differ, and that the same objects, as seen by dogs, fishes, lions, men, and locusts, are neither equal in size nor similar in shape, but vary according to the image of each object created by the particular sight that receives the impression.

50 Of the other sense organs also the same account holds good. Thus, in respect of touch, how could one maintain that creatures covered with shells, with flesh, with prickles, with feathers, with scales, are all similarly affected? And as for the sense of hearing, how could we say that its perceptions are alike in

animals with a very narrow auditory passage and those with a very wide one, or in animals with hairy ears and those with smooth ears? For, as regards this sense, even we ourselves find our hearing affected in one way when we have our ears plugged and in another way when we use them just as they are. Smell **51** also will differ because of the variety in animals. For if we ourselves are affected in one way when we have a cold and our internal phlegm is excessive, and in another when the parts about our head are filled with an excess of blood, feeling an aversion to smells which seem sweet to everyone else and regarding them as noxious, it is reasonable to suppose that animals too—since some are flaccid by nature and rich in phlegm, others rich in blood, others marked by a predominant excess of yellow or of black gall—are in each case impressed in different ways by the objects of smell. So too with the objects of taste; for some **52** animals have rough and dry tongues, others extremely moist tongues. We ourselves, too, when our tongues are very dry, in cases of fever, think the food proffered us to be earthy and ill-flavored or bitter—an affection due to the variation in the predominating juices which we are said to contain. Since, then, animals also have organs of taste which differ and which have different juices in excess, in respect of taste also they will receive different impressions of the real objects. For just as the same food when digested becomes in one place **53** a vein, in another an artery, in another a bone, in another a sinew, or some other piece of the body, displaying a different potency according to the dif-

54 ference in the parts which receive it;—and just as the same unblended water, when it is absorbed by trees, becomes in one place bark, in another branch, in another blossom, and so finally fig and quince and each of the other fruits;—and just as the single identical breath of a musician breathed into a flute becomes here a shrill note and there a deep note, and the same pressure of his hand on the lyre produces here a deep note and there a shrill note;—so likewise is it probable that the external objects appear different owing to differences in the structure of the animals which experience the sense impressions.

55 But one may learn this more clearly from the preferences and aversions of animals. Thus, sweet oil seems very agreeable to men, but intolerable to beetles and bees; and olive oil is beneficial to men, but when poured on wasps and bees it destroys them; and seawater is a disagreeable and poisonous potion

56 for men, but fish drink and enjoy it. Pigs, too, enjoy wallowing in the most stinking mire rather than in clear and clean water. And whereas some animals eat grass, others eat shrubs, others feed in the woods, others live on seeds or flesh or milk; some of them, too, prefer their food high, others like it fresh, and while some prefer it raw, others like it cooked. And so generally, the things which are agreeable to some are to others disagreeable, distasteful, and deadly.

57 Thus, quails are fattened by hemlock, and pigs by henbane; and pigs also enjoy eating salamanders, just as deer enjoy poisonous creatures, and swallows gnats. So ants and wood lice, when swallowed by men, cause distress and gripings, whereas the bear, whenever she falls sick, cures herself by licking them up. The mere touch of an oak twig paralyses the viper, **58** and that of a plane leaf the bat. The elephant flees from the ram, the lion from the cock, sea monsters from the crackle of bursting beans, and the tiger from the sound of a drum. One might, indeed, cite many more examples, but—not to seem unduly prolix— if the same things are displeasing to some but pleasing to others, and pleasure and displeasure depend upon sense impression, then animals receive different impressions from the underlying objects.

But if the same things appear different owing **59** to the variety in animals, we shall, indeed, be able to state our own impressions of the real object, but as to its essential nature we shall suspend judgment. For we cannot ourselves judge between our own impressions and those of other animals, since we ourselves are involved in the dispute and are, therefore, rather in need of a judge than competent to pass judgment ourselves. Besides, we are unable, either with or with- **60** out proof, to prefer our own impressions to those of the irrational animals. For in addition to the probability that proof is, as we shall show, a nonentity, the so-called proof itself will be either apparent to us or nonapparent. If, then, it is nonapparent, we shall not accept it with confidence; while if it is apparent to us, inasmuch as what is apparent to animals is the point in question and the proof is apparent to us who are animals, it follows that we shall have to question the proof itself as to whether it is as true

61   as it is apparent. It is, indeed, absurd to attempt to establish the matter in question by means of the matter in question, since in that case the same thing will be at once believed and disbelieved,—believed in so far as it purports to prove, but disbelieved in so far as it requires proof,—which is impossible. Consequently we shall not possess a proof which enables us to give our own sense impressions the preference over those of the so-called irrational animals. If, then, owing to the variety in animals their sense impressions differ, and it is impossible to judge between them, we must necessarily suspend judgment regarding the external underlying objects.

62   By way of superaddition, too, we draw comparisons between mankind and the so-called irrational animals in respect of their sense impressions. For, after our solid arguments, we deem it quite proper to poke fun at those conceited braggarts, the dogmatists. As a rule, our school compare the irrational

63   animals in the mass with mankind; but since the dogmatists captiously assert that the comparison is unequal, we—superadding yet more—will carry our ridicule further and base our argument on one animal only, the dog, for instance, if you like, which is held to be the most worthless of animals. For even in this case we shall find that the animals we are discussing are no wise inferior to ourselves in respect of the credibility of their impressions.

64   Now it is allowed by the dogmatists that this animal, the dog, excels us in point of sensation: as to smell it is more sensitive than we are, since by this sense it tracks beasts that it cannot see; and with its eyes it sees them more quickly than we do; and with its ears it is keen of perception. Next let us **65** proceed with the reasoning faculty. Of reason one kind is internal, implanted in the soul, the other externally expressed.* Let us consider first the internal reason. Now according to those dogmatists who are, at present, our chief opponents—I mean the Stoics— internal reason is supposed to be occupied with the following matters: the choice of things congenial and the avoidance of things alien; the knowledge of the arts contributing thereto; the apprehension of the virtues pertaining to one's proper nature and of those relating to the passions. Now the dog—the animal **66** upon which, by way of example, we have decided to base our argument—exercises choice of the congenial and avoidance of the harmful, in that it hunts after food and slinks away from a raised whip. Moreover, it possesses an art which supplies that which is congenial, namely hunting. Nor is it devoid **67** even of virtue; for certainly if justice consists in rendering to each his due, the dog, that welcomes and guards its friends and benefactors but drives off strangers and evildoers, cannot be lacking in justice. But if he possesses this virtue, then, since the virtues **68** are interdependent, he possesses also all the other virtues; and these, say the philosophers, the majority of men do not possess. That the dog is also valiant

---

*The Stoic theory of *logos* thus distinguished between its two senses— internal reason, or conception, and the enunciation of thought in the uttered *word*.

we see by the way he repels attacks, and intelligent as well, as Homer too testified* when he sang how Odysseus went unrecognized by all the people of his own household and was recognized only by the dog Argus, who neither was deceived by the bodily alterations of the hero nor had lost his original apprehensive impression, which indeed he evidently re-

69 tained better than the men. And according to Chrysippus,† who shows special interest in irrational animals, the dog even shares in the far-famed "dialectic." This person, at any rate, declares that the dog makes use of the fifth complex indemonstrable syllogism‡ when, arriving at a spot where three ways meet, after smelling at the two roads by which the quarry did not pass, he rushes off at once by the third without stopping to smell. For, says the old writer, the dog implicitly reasons thus: "The creature went either by this road, or by that, or by the other: but it did not go by this road or by that: therefore it went by the other."

70 Moreover, the dog is capable of comprehending and assuaging his own sufferings; for when a thorn has got stuck in his foot he hastens to remove it by rubbing his foot on the ground and by using his teeth. And if he has a wound anywhere, because dirty wounds are hard to cure whereas clean ones heal easily, the

---

*Odyssey, xvii. 300.

†[Ca. 280–206 B.C. Greek Stoic philosopher, considered, with Zeno, to be the founder of the Stoa academy in Athens.]

‡The Stoics had five syllogisms which they termed *anapodeictic,* or "indemonstrable," since they required no proof themselves but served to prove others. The "complex" syllogism was of the form: "Either A or B or C exists; but neither A nor B exists; therefore C exists."

dog gently licks off the pus that has gathered. Nay **71** more, the dog admirably observes the prescription of Hippocrates*: rest being what cures the foot, whenever he gets his foot hurt he lifts it up and keeps it as far as possible free from pressure. And when distressed by unwholesome humors he eats grass, by the help of which he vomits what is unwholesome and gets well again. If, then, it has been shown that **72** the animal upon which, as an example, we have based our argument not only chooses the wholesome and avoids the noxious, but also possesses an art capable of supplying what is wholesome, and is capable of comprehending and assuaging its own sufferings, and is not devoid of virtue, then—these being the things in which the perfection of internal reasons consists— the dog will be thus far perfect. And that, I suppose, is why certain of the professors of philosophy have adorned themselves with the title of this animal.

Concerning external reason, or speech, it is un- **73** necessary for the present to inquire; for it has been rejected even by some of the dogmatists as being a hindrance to the acquisition of virtue, for which reason they used to practice silence during the period of instruction; and besides, supposing that a man is dumb, no one will therefore call him irrational. But to pass over these cases, we certainly see animals— the subject of our argument—uttering quite human cries,—jays, for instance, and others. And, leaving **74** this point also aside, even if we do not understand

---

*The famous physician, of Cos (ca. 460-400 B.C.).

the utterances of the so-called irrational animals, still it is not improbable that they converse although we fail to understand them; for in fact when we listen to the talk of barbarians we do not understand it,

75 and it seems to us a kind of uniform chatter. Moreover, we hear dogs uttering one sound when they are driving people off, another when they are howling, and one sound when beaten, and a quite different sound when fawning. And so in general, in the case of all other animals as well as the dog, whoever examines the matter carefully will find a great variety of utterance according to the different circumstances, so that, in consequence, the so-called irrational animals may justly be said to participate in external

76 reason. But if they neither fall short of mankind in the accuracy of their perceptions, nor in internal reason, nor yet (to go still further) in external reason, or speech, then they will deserve no less credence than ourselves in respect of their sense impressions.

77 Probably, too, we may reach this conclusion by basing our argument on each single class of irrational animals. Thus, for example, who would deny that birds excel in quickness of wit or that they employ external reason? For they understand not only present events but future events as well, and these they foreshow to such as are able to comprehend them by means of prophetic cries as well as by other signs.

78 I have drawn this comparison (as I previously indicated) by way of superaddition, having already sufficiently proved, as I think, that we cannot prefer our own sense impressions to those of the irrational

animals. If, however, the irrational animals are not less worthy of credence than we in regard to the value of sense impressions, and their impressions vary according to the variety of animal,—then, although I shall be able to say what the nature of each of the underlying objects appears to me to be, I shall be compelled, for the reasons stated above, to suspend judgment as to its real nature.

Such, then, is the first of the modes which induce **79** suspense. The *second mode* is, as we said, that based on the differences in men; for even if we grant for the sake of argument that men are more worthy of credence than irrational animals, we shall find that even our own differences of themselves lead to suspense. For man, you know, is said to be compounded of two things, soul and body, and in both these we differ one from another.

Thus, as regards the *body,* we differ in our figures and "idiosyncrasies," or constitutional peculiarities. The body of an Indian differs in shape from that **80** of a Scythian; and it is said that what causes the variation is a difference in the predominant humors. Owing to this difference in the predominant humors the sense impressions also come to differ, as we indicated in our first argument. So too in respect of choice and avoidance of external objects men exhibit great differences: thus Indians enjoy some things, our people other things, and the enjoyment of different things is an indication that we receive varying impressions from the underlying objects. In respect of our "idiosyncrasies," our differences are such that **81** some of us digest the flesh of oxen more easily than rockfish, or get diarrhea from the weak wine of Lesbos. An old wife of Attica, they say, swallowed with impunity thirty drams of hemlock, and Lysis took four drams of poppy juice without hurt.

82 Demophon, Alexander's butler, used to shiver when he was in the sun or in a hot bath, but felt warm in the shade: Athenagoras the Argive took no hurt from the stings of scorpions and poisonous spiders; and the Psyllaeans,* as they are called, are not harmed

83 by bites from snakes and asps, nor are the Tentyritae† of Egypt harmed by the crocodile. Further, those Ethiopians who live beyong Lake Meroë‡ on the banks of the river Astapous eat with impunity scorpions, snakes, and the like. Rufinus of Chalcis when he drank hellebore neither vomited nor suffered at all from the purging, but swallowed and digested it

84 just like any other ordinary drink. Chrysermus the Herophilean doctor was liable to get a heart attack if ever he took pepper; and Soterichus the surgeon was seized with diarrhea whenever he smelled fried sprats. Andron the Argive was so immune from thirst that he actually traversed the waterless country of Libya without needing a drink. Tiberius Caesar could see in the dark; and Aristotle tells of a Thasian who fancied that the image of a man was continually going in front of him.

85 Seeing, then, that men vary so much in body—

---

*A tribe of N. Africa.
†Tentyra was a town in Upper Egypt.
†In S. Egypt.

to content ourselves with but a few instances of the many collected by the dogmatists,—men probably also differ from one another in respect of the *soul* itself; for the body is a kind of expression of the soul, as in fact is proved by the science of physiognomy. But the greatest proof of the vast and endless differences in men's intelligence is the discrepancy in the statements of the dogmatists concerning the right objects of choice and avoidance, as well as other things. Regarding this the poets, too, have expressed **86** themselves fittingly. Thus Pindar says:

> The crowns and trophies of his storm-foot steeds
> Give joy to one; yet others find it joy
> To dwell in gorgeous chambers gold-bedeckt;
> Some even take delight in voyaging
> O'er ocean's billows in a speeding barque.

And the poet* says: "One thing is pleasing to one man, another thing to another." Tragedy, too, is full of such sayings; for example:

> Were fair and wise the same thing unto all
> There had been no contentious quarrelling.

And again:

> 'Tis strange that the same thing abhorr'd by some
> Should give delight to others.

---

*See Homer, *Odyssey,* xiv. 228.

87 Seeing, then, that choice and avoidance depend on pleasure and displeasure, while pleasure and displeasure depend on sensation and sense impression, whenever some men choose the very things which are avoided by others, it is logical for us to conclude that they are also differently affected by the same things, since otherwise they would all alike have chosen or avoided the same things. But if the same objects affect men differently owing to the differences in the men, then, on this ground also, we shall reasonably be led to suspension of judgment. For while we are, no doubt, able to state what each of the underlying objects appears to be, relatively to each difference, we are incapable of explaining what it **88** is in reality. For we shall have to believe either all men or some. But if we believe all, we shall be attempting the impossible and accepting contradictories; and if some, let us be told whose opinions we are to endorse. For the Platonist will say "Plato's"; the Epicurean, "Epicurus's"; and so on with the rest; and thus by their unsettled disputations they will bring **89** us round again to a state of suspense. Moreover, he who maintains that we ought to assent to the majority is making a childish proposal, since no one is able to visit the whole of mankind and determine what pleases the majority of them; for there may possibly be races of whom we know nothing amongst whom conditions rare with us are common, and conditions common with us rare,—possibly, for instance, most of them feel no pain from the bites of spiders, though a few on rare occasions feel such pain; and so likewise with the rest of the "idiosyncrasies" mentioned above. Necessarily, therefore, the differences in men afford a further reason for bringing in suspension of judgment.

When the dogmatists—a self-loving class of **90** men—assert that in judging things they ought to prefer themselves to other people, we know that their claim is absurd; for they themselves are a party to the controversy; and if, when judging appearances, they have already given the preference to themselves, then, by thus entrusting themselves with the judgment, they are begging the question before the judgment is begun. Nevertheless, in order that we may arrive at suspen- **91** sion of judgment by basing our argument on one person—such as, for example, their visionary "sage"— we adopt the mode which comes third in order.

This *third mode* is, we say, based on differences in the senses. That the senses differ from one another is obvious. Thus, to the eye paintings seem to have **92** recesses and projections, but not so to the touch. Honey, too, seems to some pleasant to the tongue but unpleasant to the eyes; so that it is impossible to say whether it is absolutely pleasant or unpleasant. The same is true of sweet oil, for it pleases the sense of smell but displeases the taste. So too with spurge: **93** since it pains the eyes but causes no pain to any other part of the body, we cannot say whether, in its real nature, it is absolutely painful or painless to bodies. Rainwater, too, is beneficial to the eyes but roughens the windpipe and the lungs; as also does olive oil, though it mollifies the epidermis. The cramp-fish, also, when applied to the extremities produces cramp, but it can be applied to the rest of the body without hurt. Consequently we are unable to say what is the real nature of each of these things, although it is possible to say what each thing at the moment appears to be.

94   A longer list of examples might be given, but to avoid prolixity, in view of the plan of our treatise, we will say just this. Each of the phenomena perceived by the senses seems to be a complex: the apple, for example, seems smooth, odorous, sweet, and yellow. But it is nonevident whether it really possesses these qualities only; or whether it has but one quality but appears varied owing to the varying structure of the sense organs; or whether, again, it has more qualities than are apparent, some of which elude our per-

95   ception. That the apple has but one quality might be argued from what we said above regarding the food absorbed by bodies, and the water sucked up by trees, and the breath in flutes and pipes and similar instruments; for the apple likewise may be all of one sort but appear different owing to differences in the sense organs in which perception takes place. And

96   that the apple may possibly possess more qualities than those apparent to us we argue in this way. Let us imagine a man who possesses from birth the senses of touch, taste, and smell, but can neither hear nor see. This man, then, will assume that nothing visual or audible has any existence, but only those three kinds of qualities which he is able to apprehend.

97   Possibly, then, we also, having only our five senses, perceive only such of the apple's qualities as we are capable of apprehending; and possibly it may possess other underlying qualities which affect other sense organs, though we, not being endowed with those organs, fail to apprehend the sense objects which come through them.

"But," it may be objected, "nature made the senses **98** commensurate with the objects of sense." What kind of "nature"? we ask, seeing that there exists so much unresolved controversy amongst the dogmatists concerning the reality which belongs to nature. For he who decides the question as to the existence of nature will be discredited by them if he is an ordinary person, while if he is a philosopher he will be a party to the controversy and therefore himself subject to judgment and not a judge. If, however, it is possible that **99** only those qualities which we seem to perceive subsist in the apple, or that a greater number subsist, or, again, that not even the qualities which affect us subsist, then it will be nonevident to us what the nature of the apple really is. And the same argument applies to all the other objects of sense. But if the senses do not apprehend external objects, neither can the mind apprehend them; hence, because of this argument also, we shall be driven, it seems, to suspend judgment regarding the external underlying objects.

In order that we may finally reach suspension **100** by basing our argument on each sense singly, or even by disregarding the senses, we further adopt the *fourth mode* of suspension. This is the mode based, as we say, on the "circumstances," meaning by "circumstances" conditions or dispositions. And this mode, we say, deals with states that are natural or unnatural, with waking or sleeping, with conditions due to age, motion or rest, hatred or love, emptiness or fullness, drunkenness or soberness, predispositions, confidence **101** or fear, grief or joy. Thus, according as the mental state is natural or unnatural, objects produce dissimilar impressions, as when men in a frenzy or in a state of ecstasy believe they hear demons' voices, while we do not. Similarly they often say that they perceive an odor of storax or frankincense, or some such scent, and many other things, though we fail to perceive them. Also, the same water which feels very hot when poured on inflamed spots seems lukewarm to us. And the same coat which seems of a bright yellow color to men with bloodshot eyes does not appear so to me. And the same honey seems **102** to me sweet, but bitter to men with jaundice. Now should anyone say that it is an intermixture of certain humors which produces in those who are in an unnatural state improper impressions from the underlying objects, we have to reply that, since healthy persons also have mixed humors, these humors too are capable of causing the external objects—which really are such as they appear to those who are said to be in an unnatural state—to appear other than **103** they are to healthy persons. For to ascribe the power of altering the underlying objects to those humors, and not to these, is purely fanciful; since just as healthy men are in a state that is natural for the healthy but unnatural for the sick, so also sick men are in a state that is unnatural for the healthy but natural for the sick, so that to these last also we must give credence as being, relatively speaking, in a natural state.

Sleeping and waking, too, give rise to different **104** impressions, since we do not imagine when awake what we imagine in sleep, nor when asleep what we imagine when awake; so that the existence or non-existence of our impressions is not absolute but relative, being in relation to our sleeping or waking condition. Probably, then, in dreams we see things which to our waking state are unreal, although not wholly unreal; for they exist in our dreams, just as waking realities exist although nonexistent in dreams.

Age is another cause of difference. For the same **105** air seems chilly to the old but mild to those in their prime; and the same color appears faint to older men but vivid to those in their prime; and similarly the same sound seems to the former faint, but to the latter clearly audible. Moreover, those who differ in **106** age are differently moved in respect of choice and avoidance. For whereas children—to take a case—are all eagerness for balls and hoops, men in their prime choose other things, and old men yet others. And from this we conclude that differences in age also cause different impressions to be produced by the same underlying objects.

Another cause why the real objects appear dif- **107** ferent lies in motion and rest. For those objects which, when we are standing still, we see to be motionless, we imagine to be in motion when we are sailing past them.

108 Love and hatred are a cause, as when some have an extreme aversion to pork while others greatly enjoy eating it. Hence, too, Menander said:

> Mark now his visage, what a change is there
> Since he has come to this! How bestial!
> 'Tis actions fair that make the fairest face.

Many lovers, too, who have ugly mistresses think them most beautiful.

109 Hunger and satiety are a cause; for the same food seems agreeable to the hungry but disagreeable to the sated.

Drunkenness and soberness are a cause; since actions which we think shameful when sober do not seem shameful to us when drunk.

110 Predispositions are a cause; for the same wine which seems sour to those who have previously eaten dates or figs, seems sweet to those who have just consumed nuts or chickpeas; and the vestibule of the bathhouse, which warms those entering from outside, chills those coming out of the bathroom if they stop long in it.

111 Fear and boldness are a cause; as what seems to the coward fearful and formidable does not seem so in the least to the bold man.

Grief and joy are a cause; since the same affairs are burdensome to those in grief but delightful to those who rejoice.

Seeing then that the dispositions also are the **112**
cause of so much disagreement, and that men are
differently disposed at different times, although, no
doubt, it is easy to say what nature each of the
underlying objects appears to each man to possess,
we cannot go on to say what its real nature is, since
the disagreement admits in itself of no settlement.
For the person who tries to settle it is either in one
of the aforementioned dispositions or in no disposition whatsoever. But to declare that he is in no
disposition at all—as, for instance, neither in health
nor sickness, neither in motion nor at rest, of no
definite age, and devoid of all the other dispositions
as well—is the height of absurdity. And if he is to
judge the sense impressions while he is in some one
disposition, he will be a party to the disagreement, **113**
and, moreover, he will not be an impartial judge
of the external underlying objects owing to his being
confused by the dispositions in which he is placed.
The waking person, for instance, cannot compare
the impressions of sleepers with those of men awake,
nor the sound person those of the sick with those
of the sound; for we assent more readily to things
present, which affect us in the present, than to things
not present.

In another way, too, the disagreement of such **114**
impressions is incapable of settlement. For he who
prefers one impression to another, or one "circumstance" to another, does so either uncritically and
without proof or critically and with proof; but he
can do this neither without these means (for then

he would be discredited) nor with them. For if he is to pass judgment on the impressions he must

115 certainly judge them by a criterion; this criterion, then, he will declare to be true, or else false. But if false, he will be discredited; whereas, if he shall declare it to be true, he will be stating that the criterion is true either without proof or with proof. But if without proof, he will be discredited; and if with proof, it will certainly be necessary for the proof also to be true, to avoid being discredited. Shall he, then, affirm the truth of the proof adopted to establish the criterion after having judged it or without judging

116 it? If without judging, he will be discredited; but if after judging, plainly he will say that he has judged it by a criterion; and of that criterion we shall ask for a proof, and of that proof again a criterion. For the proof always requires a criterion to confirm it, and the criterion also a proof to demonstrate its truth; and neither can a proof be sound without the previous existence of a true criterion nor can the criterion be true without the previous confirmation of the proof.

117 So in this way both the criterion and the proof are involved in the circular process of reasoning, and thereby both are found to be untrustworthy; for since each of them is dependent on the credibility of the other, the one is lacking in credibility just as much as the other. Consequently, if a man can prefer one impression to another neither without a proof and a criterion nor with them, then the different impressions due to the differing conditions will admit of no settlement; so that as a result of this mode also we are brought to suspend judgment regarding the nature of external realities.

The *fifth argument* (or *trope*) is that based on **118** positions, distances, and locations; for owing to each of these the same objects appear different; for example, the same porch when viewed from one of its corners appears curtailed, but viewed from the middle symmetrical on all sides; and the same ship seems at a distance to be small and stationary, but from close at hand large and in motion; and the same tower from a distance appears round but from a near point quadrangular.

These effects are due to distances; among effects **119** due to locations are the following: the light of a lamp appears dim in the sun but bright in the dark; and the same oar bent when in the water but straight when out of the water; and the egg soft when inside the fowl but hard when in the air; and the jacinth fluid when in the lynx but hard when in the air; and the coral soft when in the sea but hard when in the air; and sound seems to differ in quality according as it is produced in a pipe, or in a flute, or simply in the air.

Effects due to positions are such as these: the **120** same painting when laid flat appears smooth, but when inclined forward at a certain angle it seems to have recesses and prominences. The necks of doves, also, appear different in hue according to the differences in the angle of inclination.

Since, then, all apparent objects are viewed in **121** a certain place, and from a certain distance, or in a certain position, and each of these conditions produces a great divergency in the sense impressions, as we mentioned above, we shall be compelled by this mode also to end up in suspension of judgment. For in fact anyone who purposes to give the preference to any of these impressions will be attempting the

122 impossible. For if he shall deliver his judgment simply and without proof, he will be discredited; and should he, on the other hand, desire to adduce proof, he will confute himself if he says that the proof is false, while if he asserts that the proof is true he will be asked for a proof of its truth, and again for a proof of this latter proof, since it also must be true, and so on *ad infinitum.* But to produce proofs to infinity

123 is impossible; so that neither by the use of proofs will he be able to prefer one sense impression to another. If, then, one cannot hope to pass judgment on the aforementioned impressions either with or without proof, the conclusion we are driven to is suspension; for while we can, no doubt, state the nature which each object appears to possess as viewed in a certain position or at a certain distance or in a certain place, what its real nature is we are, for the foregoing reasons, unable to declare.

124 The *sixth mode* is that based on admixtures, by which we conclude that, because none of the real objects affects our senses by itself but always in conjunction with something else, though we may possibly be able to state the nature of the resultant mixture formed by the external object and that along with which it is perceived, we shall not be able to say what is the exact nature of the external reality in itself. That none of the external objects affects our senses by itself but always in conjunction with something else, and that, in consequence, it assumes a different appearance, is, I imagine, quite obvious. Thus, our own complexion is of one hue in warm **125** air, of another in cold, and we should not be able to say what our complexion really is, but only what it looks like in conjunction with each of these conditions. And the same sound appears of one sort in conjunction with rare air and of another sort with dense air; and odors are more pungent in a hot bathroom or in the sun than in chilly air; and a body is light when immersed in water but heavy when surrounded by air.

But to pass on from the subject of external ad- **126** mixture,—our eyes contain within themselves both membranes and liquids. Since, then, the objects of vision are not perceived apart from these, they will not be apprehended with exactness; for what we perceive is the resultant mixture, and because of this the sufferers from jaundice see everything yellow, and those with bloodshot eyes reddish like blood. And since the same sound seems of one quality in open places, of another in narrow and winding places, and different in clear air and in murky air, it is probable that we do not apprehend the sound in its real purity; for the ears have crooked and narrow passages, which are also befogged by various vaporous effluvia which are said to be emitted by the regions of the head. Moreover, since there reside substances in the nostrils **127** and in the organs of taste, we apprehend the objects of taste and smell in conjunction with these and not in their real purity. So that, because of these admixtures, the senses do not apprehend the exact quality of the external real objects.

128 Nor yet does the mind apprehend it, since, in the first place, its guides, which are the senses, go wrong; and probably, too, the mind itself adds a certain admixture of its own to the messages conveyed by the senses; for we observe that there are certain humors present in each of the regions which the dogmatists regard as the seat of the "ruling principle"—whether it be the brain or the heart, or in whatever part of the creature one chooses to locate it. Thus, according to this mode also we see that, owing to our inability to make any statement about the real nature of external objects, we are compelled to suspend judgment.

129 The *seventh mode* is that based, as we said, on the quantity and constitution of the underlying objects, meaning generally by "constitution" the manner of composition. And it is evident that by this mode also we are compelled to suspend judgment concerning the real nature of the objects. Thus, for example, the filings of a goat's horns appear white when viewed simply by themselves and without combination, but when combined in the substance of the horn they look black. And silver filings appear black when they are by themselves, but when united to the whole mass **130** they are sensed as white. And chips of the marble of Taenarum seem white when planed, but in combination with the whole block they appear yellow. And pebbles when scattered apart appear rough, but when combined in a heap they produce the sensation of softness. And hellebore if applied in a fine and powdery state produces suffocation, but not so when it is coarse. And wine strengthens us when drunk **131** in moderate quantity, but when too much is taken it paralyzes the body. So likewise food exhibits different effects according to the quantity consumed; for instance, it frequently upsets the body with indigestion and attacks of purging because of the large **132** quantity taken. Therefore in these cases, too, we shall be able to describe the quality of the shaving of the horn and of the compound made up of many shavings, and that of the particle of silver and of the compound of many particles, and that of the sliver of Taenarean marble and of the compound of many such small pieces, and the relative qualities of the pebbles, the hellebore, the wine, and the food,— but when it comes to the independent and real nature of the objects, this we shall be unable to describe because of the divergency in the sense impressions which is due to the combinations.

As a general rule, it seems that wholesome things **133** become harmful when used in immoderate quantities, and things that seem hurtful when taken to excess cause no harm when in minute quantities. What we observe in regard to the effects of medicines is the best evidence in support of our statement; for there the exact blending of the simple drugs makes the compound wholesome, but when the slightest over-

sight is made in the measuring, as sometimes happens, the compound is not only unwholesome but fre-
134 quently even most harmful and deleterious. Thus the argument from quantities and compositions causes confusion as to the real nature of the external substances. Probably, therefore, this mode also will bring us round to a suspension of judgment, as we are unable to make any absolute statement concerning the real nature of external objects.

135 The *eighth mode* is that based on relativity; and by it we conclude that, since all things are relative, we shall suspend judgment as to what things are absolutely and really existent. But this point we must notice—that here as elsewhere we use the term "are" for the term "appear," and what we virtually mean is "all things appear relative." And this statement is twofold, implying, firstly, relation to the thing which judges (for the external object which is judged appears in relation to that thing), and, in a second sense, relation to the accompanying percepts, for instance
136 the right side in relation to the left. Indeed, we have already argued that all things are relative—for example, with respect to the thing which judges, it is in relation to some one particular animal or man or sense that each object appears, and in relation to such and such a circumstance; and with respect to the concomitant percepts, each object appears in relation to some one particular admixture or mode or combination or quantity or position.

137 There are also special arguments to prove the relativity of all things, in this way: Do things which exist "differentially" differ from relative things or not? If they do not differ, then they too are relative; but if they differ, then, since everything which differs is relative to something (for it has its name from its relation to that from which it differs), things which exist differently are relative. Again,—of existing things **138** some, according to the dogmatists, are *summa genera,* others *infimae species,* others both genera and species; and all these are relative; therefore all things are relative. Further, some existing things are "preevident," as they say, others nonevident; and the apparent things are significant, but the nonevident signified by the apparent; for according to them "the things apparent are the vision of the nonevident." But the significant and the signified are relative; therefore all things are relative. Moreover, some existent things **139** are similar, others dissimilar, and some equal, others unequal; and these are relative; therefore all things are relative. And even he who asserts that not all things are relative confirms the relativity of all things, since by his arguments against us he shows that the very statement "not all things are relative" is relative to ourselves, and not universal.

When, however, we have thus established that **140** all things are relative, we are plainly left with the conclusion that we shall not be able to state what is the nature of each of the objects in its own real purity, but only what nature it appears to possess in its relative character. Hence it follows that we must suspend judgment concerning the real nature of the objects.

141   The *mode* which, as we said, comes *ninth* in order is based on constancy or rarity of occurrence, and we shall explain it as follows. The sun is, of course, much more amazing than a comet; yet, because we see the sun constantly but the comet rarely, we are so amazed by the comet that we even regard it as a divine portent, while the sun causes no amazement at all. If, however, we were to conceive of the sun as appearing but rarely and setting rarely, and illuminating everything all at once and throwing everything into shadow suddenly, then we should

142   experience much amazement at the sight. An earthquake also does not cause the same alarm in those who experience it for the first time and those who have grown accustomed to such things. How much amazement, also, does the sea excite in the man who sees it for the first time! And indeed the beauty of a human body thrills us more at the first sudden view than when it becomes a customary spectacle. Rare things too we count as precious, but not what

143   is familiar to us and easily got. Thus, if we should suppose water to be rare, how much more precious it would appear to us than all the things which are accounted precious! Or if we should imagine gold to be simply scattered in quantities over the earth like stones, to whom do we suppose it would then be precious and worth hoarding?

144   Since then, owing to the frequency or rarity of their occurrence, the same things seem at one time to be amazing or precious and at another time nothing of the sort, we infer that though we shall be able perhaps to say what nature appears to belong to each of these things in virtue of its frequent or rare occurrence, we are not able to state what nature absolutely belongs to each of the external objects. So because of this mode also we suspend judgment regarding them.

There is a *tenth mode,* which is mainly concerned **145** with ethics, being based on rules of conduct, habits, laws, legendary beliefs, and dogmatic conceptions. A rule of conduct is a choice of a way of life, or of a particular action, adopted by one person or many—by Diogenes,* for instance, or the Laconians. A law is a written contract amongst the members **146** of a state, the transgressor of which is punished. A habit or custom (the terms are equivalent) is the joint adoption of a certain kind of action by a number of men, the transgressor of which is not actually punished; for example, the law proscribes adultery, and custom with us forbids intercourse with a woman in public. Legendary belief is the acceptance of unhis- **147** torical and fictitious events, such as, amongst others, the legends about Cronos; for these stories win credence with many. Dogmatic conception is the acceptance of a fact which seems to be established by analogy or some form of demonstration, as, for example, that atoms are the elements of existing things, or homoeomeries, or *minima,* or something else.

And each of these we oppose now to itself, and **148** now to each of the others. For example, we oppose

---

*[The Cynic philosopher [ca. 400-325 B.C.].

149 habit to habit in this way: some of the Ethiopians tattoo their children, but we do not; and while the Persians think it seemly to wear a brightly dyed dress reaching to the feet, we think it unseemly; and whereas the Indians have intercourse with their women in public, most other races regard this as shameful. And law we oppose to law in this way: among the Romans the man who renounces his father's property does not pay his father's debts, but among the Rhodians he always pays them; and among the Scythian Tauri* it was a law that strangers should be sacrificed to Artemis, but with us it is forbidden to slay a human

150 being at the altar. And we oppose rule of conduct to rule of conduct, as when we oppose the rule of Diogenes to that of Aristippus or that of the Laconians to that of the Italians. And we oppose legendary belief to legendary belief when we say that whereas in one story the father of men and gods is alleged to be Zeus, in another he is Oceanos—"Ocean sire of the gods, and Tethys the mother that bare them."

151 And we oppose dogmatic conceptions to one another when we say that some declare that there is one element only, others an infinite number; some that the soul is mortal, others that it is immortal; and some that human affairs are controlled by divine providence, others without providence.

152 And we oppose habit to the other things, as for instance to law when we say that amongst the Persians it is the habit to indulge in intercourse with males,

---

*I.e., inhabitants of the Crimea.

but amongst the Romans it is forbidden by law to do so; and that, whereas with us adultery is forbidden, amongst the Massagetae* it is traditionally regarded as an indifferent custom, as Eudoxus of Cnidos† relates in the first book of his *Travels;* and that, whereas intercourse with a mother is forbidden in our country, in Persia it is the general custom to form such marriages; and also among the Egyptians men marry their sisters, a thing forbidden by law amongst us. And **153** habit is opposed to rule of conduct when, whereas most men have intercourse with their own wives in retirement, Crates‡ did it in public with Hipparchia; and Diogenes went about with one shoulder bare, whereas we dress in the customary manner. It is opposed also to legendary belief, as when the legends **154** say that Cronos devoured his own children, though it is our habit to protect our children; and whereas it is customary with us to revere the gods as being good and immune from evil, they are presented by the poets as suffering wounds and envying one another. And habit is opposed to dogmatic conception when, **155** whereas it is our habit to pray to the gods for good things, Epicurus declares that the divinity pays no heed to us; and when Aristippus§ considers the wearing of feminine attire a matter of indifference, though we consider it a disgraceful thing.

And we oppose rule of conduct to law when, **156**

---

*[An ancient Indo-European tribe of Russian Turkestan.]

†Fl. ca. 360 B.C., famed as astronomer, geometer, legislator, and physician.

‡A cynic philosopher, ca. 320 B.C.

§[Ca. 435–366 B.C. Greek philosopher and founder of the Cyrenaic school of hedonism.]

though there is a law which forbids the striking of a free or well-born man, the pancratiasts strike one another because of the rule of life they follow; and when, though homicide is forbidden, gladiators

157 destroy one another for the same reason. And we oppose legendary belief to rule of conduct when we say that the legends relate that Heracles in the house of Omphale "toiled at the spinning of wool, enduring slavery's burden," and did things which no one would have chosen to do even in a moderate degree, whereas the rule of life of Heracles was a noble one. And

158 we oppose rule of conduct to dogmatic conception when, whereas athletes covet glory as something good and for its sake undertake a toilsome rule of life, many of the philosophers dogmatically assert that

159 glory is a worthless thing. And we oppose law to legendary belief when the poets represent the gods as commiting adultery and practicing intercourse with males, whereas the law with us forbids such actions;

160 and we oppose it to dogmatic conception when Chrysippus says that intercourse with mothers or sisters is a thing indifferent, whereas the law forbids such

161 things. And we oppose legendary belief to dogmatic conception when the poets say that Zeus came down and had intercourse with mortal women, but amongst the dogmatists it is held that such a thing is impossible;

162 and again, when the poet relates that because of his grief for Sarpedon Zeus "let fall upon the earth great gouts of blood," whereas it is a dogma of the philosophers that the deity is impassive; and when these same philosophers demolish the legend of the hippo-centaurs, and offer us the hippocentaur as a type of unreality.

We might indeed have taken many other **163** examples in connection with each of the antitheses above mentioned; but in a concise account like ours, these will be sufficient. Only, since by means of this mode also so much divergency is shown to exist in objects, we shall not be able to state what character belongs to the object in respect of its real essence, but only what belongs to it in respect of this particular rule of conduct, or law, or habit, and so on with each of the rest. So because of this mode also we are compelled to suspend judgment regarding the real nature of external objects. And thus by means of all the ten modes we are finally led to suspension of judgment.

Chapter XV. Of the Five Modes

The later skeptics hand down five modes leading to **164** suspension, namely these: the first based on discrepancy, the second on regress *ad infinitum,* the third on relativity, the fourth on hypothesis, the fifth on circular reasoning. That based on discrepancy leads **165** us to find that with regard to the object presented there has arisen both amongst ordinary people and amongst the philosophers an interminable conflict because of which we are unable either to choose a thing or reject it, and so fall back on suspension. The mode based upon regress *ad infinitum* is that **166** whereby we assert that the thing adduced as a proof of the matter proposed needs a further proof, and this again another, and so on *ad infinitum,* so that the consequence is suspension, as we possess no start-

167 ing point for our argument. The mode based upon relativity, as we have already said, is that whereby the object has such or such an appearance in relation to the subject judging and to the concomitant per-cepts, but as to its real nature we suspend judgment.

168 We have the mode based on hypothesis when the dogmatists, being forced to recede *ad infinitum,* take as their starting point something which they do not establish by argument but claim to assume as granted simply and without demonstration. The mode of

169 circular reasoning is the form used when the proof itself which ought to establish the matter of inquiry requires confirmation derived from that matter; in this case, being unable to assume either in order to establish the other, we suspend judgment about both.

That every matter of inquiry admits of being brought under these modes we shall show briefly in

170 this way. The matter proposed is either a sense object or a thought object, but whichever it is, it is an object of controversy; for some say that only sensibles are true, others only intelligibles, others that some sensible and some intelligible objects are true. Will they then assert that the controversy can or cannot be decided? If they say it cannot, we have it granted that we must suspend judgment; for concerning matters of dispute which admit of no decision it is impossible to make an assertion. But if they say it can be decided,

171 we ask by what is it to be decided. For example,

in the case of the sense object (for we shall base our argument on it first), is it to be decided by a sense object or a thought object? For if they say a sense object, since we are inquiring about sensibles that object itself also will require another to confirm it; and if that too is to be a sense object, it likewise will require another for its confirmation, and so on *ad infinitum.* And if the sense object shall have to be decided by a thought object, then, since thought **172** objects also are controverted, this being an object of thought will need examination and confirmation. Whence then will it gain confirmation? If from an intelligible object, it will suffer a similar regress *ad infinitum;* and if from a sensible object, since an intelligible was adduced to establish the sensible and a sensible to establish the intelligible, the mode of circular reasoning is brought in.

If, however, our disputant, by way of escape **173** from this conclusion, should claim to assume as granted and without demonstration some postulate for the demonstration of the next steps of his argument, then the mode of hypothesis will be brought in, which allows no escape. For if the author of the hypothesis is worthy of credence, we shall be no less worthy of credence every time that we make the opposite hypothesis. Moreover, if the author of the hypothesis assumes what is true he causes it to be suspected by assuming it by hypothesis rather than after proof; while if it is false, the foundation of his argument will be rotten. Further, if hypothesis con- **174** duces at all to proof, let the subject of inquiry itself be assumed and not some other thing which is merely a means to establish the actual subject of the argument; but if it is absurd to assume the subject of inquiry, it will also be absurd to assume that upon which it depends.

175 It is also plain that all sensibles ar erelative; for they are relative to those who have the sensations. Therefore it is apparent that whatever sensible object is presented can easily be referred to one of the five modes. And concerning the intelligible object we argue similarly. For if it should be said that it is a matter of unsettled controversy, the necessity of our **176** suspending judgment will be granted. And if, on the other hand, the controversy admits of decision, then if the decision rests on an intelligible object we shall be driven to the regress *ad infinitum,* and to circular reasoning if it rests on a sensible; for since the sensible again is controverted and cannot be decided by means of itself because of the regress *ad infinitum,* it will require the intelligible object, just as also the intel- **177** ligible will require the sensible. For these reasons, again, he who assumes anything by hypothesis will be acting illogically. Moreover, objects of thought, or intelligibles, are relative; for they are so named on account of their relation to the person thinking, and if they had really possessed the nature they are said to possess, there would have been no controversy about them. Thus the intelligible also is referred to the five modes, so that in all cases we are compelled to suspend judgment concerning the object presented.

Such then are the five modes handed down

amongst the later skeptics; but they propound these not by way of superseding the ten modes but in order to expose the rashness of the dogmatists with more variety and completeness by means of the five in conjunction with the ten.

CHAPTER XVI. OF THE TWO MODES

They hand down also *two* other *modes* leading to **178** suspension of judgment. Since every object of apprehension seems to be apprehended either through itself or through another object, by showing that nothing is apprehended either through itself or through another thing, they introduce doubt, as they suppose, about everything. That nothing is apprehended through itself is plain, they say, from the controversy which exists amongst the physicists regarding, I imagine, all things, both sensibles and intelligibles; which controversy admits of no settlement because we can neither employ a sensible nor an intelligible criterion, since every criterion we may adopt is controverted and therefore discredited. And the reason why they do not allow that anything is **179** apprehended through something else is this: If that through which an object is apprehended must always itself be apprehended through some other thing, one is involved in a process of circular reasoning or in regress *ad infinitum*. And if, on the other hand, one should choose to assume that the thing through which another object is apprehended is itself apprehended through itself, this is refuted by the fact that, for the reasons already stated, nothing is apprehended through itself. But as to how what conflicts with itself can possibly be apprehended either through itself or through some other thing we remain in doubt, so long as the criterion of truth or of apprehension is not apparent, and signs, even apart from demonstration, are rejected, as we shall discover in our next book.

For the present, however, it will suffice to have said thus much concerning the modes leading to suspension of judgment.

CHAPTER XVII. OF THE MODES BY WHICH THE ETIOLOGISTS ARE CONFUTED

180 Just as we teach the traditional modes leading to suspense of judgment, so likewise some skeptics propound modes by which we express doubt about the particular "etiologies", or theories of causation, and thus pull up the dogmatists because of the special pride they take in these theories. Thus Aenesidemus furnishes us with *eight modes* by which, as he thinks, he tests and exposes the unsoundness of every dog- **181** matic theory of causation. Of these the first, he says, is that which shows that, since etiology as a whole deals with the nonapparent, it is unconfirmed by any agreed evidence derived from appearances. The second mode shows how often, when there is ample scope for ascribing the object of investigation to a variety of causes, some of them account for it one **182** way only. The third shows how to orderly events they assign causes which exhibit no order. The fourth shows how, when they have grasped the way in which appearances occur, they assume that they have also apprehended how nonapparent things occur, whereas, though the nonapparent may possibly be realized in a similar way to the appearances, possibly they may not be realized in a similar way but in a peculiar way of their own. In the fifth mode it is shown how **183** practically all these theorists assign causes according to their own particular hypotheses about the elements, and not according to any commonly agreed methods. In the sixth it is shown how they frequently admit only such facts as can be explained by their own theories, and dismiss facts which conflict therewith though possessing equal probability. The seventh **184** shows how they often assign causes which conflict not only with appearances but also with their own hypotheses. The eighth shows that often, when there is equal doubt about things seemingly apparent and things under investigation, they base their doctrine about things equally doubtful upon things equally doubtful. Nor is it impossible, he adds, that the over- **185** throw of some of their theories of causation should be referred to certain mixed modes which are dependent on the foregoing.

Possibly, too, the five modes of suspension may suffice as against the etiologies. For if a person propounds a cause, it will either be or not be in accord with all the philosophical systems and with skepticism and with appearances. Probably, however, it is impracticable to propound a cause in accord

186 with all of these, since all things, whether apparent or nonevident, are matters of controversy. But if, on the other hand, the cause propounded be not in accord therewith, the theorist will be asked in turn for the cause of this cause, and if he assumes an apparent cause for an apparent, or a nonevident for a nonevident, he will be involved in the regress *ad infinitum,* or reduced to arguing in a circle if he grounds each cause in turn on another. And if at any point he makes a stand, either he will state that the cause is well grounded so far as relates to the previous admissions, thus introducing relativity and destroying its claim to absolute reality, or he will make some assumption *ex hypothesi* and will be stopped by us. So by these modes also it is, no doubt, possible to expose the rashness of the dogmatists in their etiologies.

Chapter XVIII. Of the Skeptic Expressions or Formulae

187 And because when we make use of these modes and those which lead to suspension of judgment we give utterance to certain expressions indicative of our skeptical attitude and tone of mind—such as "Not more," "Nothing must be determined," and others of the kind—it will be our next task to discuss these in order. So let us begin with the expression "Not more."

CHAPTER XIX. OF THE EXPRESSION "NOT MORE"

This expression, then, we sometimes enunciate in the **188** form I have stated but sometimes in the form "Nowise more." For we do not, as some suppose, adopt the form "Not more" in specific inquiries and "Nowise more" in generic inquiries, but we enunciate both "Not more" and "Nowise more" indifferently, and we shall discuss them now as identical expressions. This expression, then, is elliptical. For just as when we say "a double" we are implicitly saying "a double hearth,"* and when we say "a square" we are implicitly saying "a square roadway," so when we say "Not more" we are implicitly saying "Not this more than that, up than down." Some of the skeptics, however, in place of the "Not" adopt the form "(For) what **189** this more than that," taking the "what" to denote, in this case, cause, so that the meaning is "For what reason this more than that?" And it is common practice to use questions instead of assertions, as for example—"The bride of Zeus, what mortal knows her not?" And also assertions in the place of questions; for instance—"I am inquiring where Dion lives," and "I ask you what reason there is for showing surprise at a poet." And further, the use of "What" instead of "For what reason" is found in Menander, "(For) what was I left behind?" And the expression "Not **190** more this than that" indicates also our feeling, whereby we come to equipoise because of the equipollence

---

*(Perhaps) a two-storeyed house [taking "hearth" as synecdoche for "house"].

71

of the opposed objects; and by "equipollence" we mean equality in respect of what seems probable to us, and by "opposed" we mean in general conflicting, and by "equipoise" refusal of assent to either alternative.

191 Then as to the formula 'Nowise more," even though it exhibits the character of a form of assent or of denial, we do not employ it this way, but we take it in a loose and inexact sense, either in place of a question or in place of the phrase "I know not to which of these things I ought to assent, and to which I ought not." For our aim is to indicate what appears to us; while as to the expression by which we indicate this we are indifferent. This point, too, should be noticed—that we utter the expression "Nowise more" not as positively affirming that it really is true and certain, but as stating in regard to it also what appears to us.

Chapter XX. Of "Aphasia" or Nonassertion

192 Concerning nonassertion what we say is this. The term "assertion" has two senses, general and special; used in the general sense it indicates affirmation or negation, as for example "It is day," "It is not day"; in its special sense it indicates affirmation only, and in this sense negations are not termed assertions. Nonassertion, then, is avoidance of assertion in the general sense in which it is said to include both affirmation and negation, so that nonassertion is a mental condition of ours because of which we refuse either to affirm or deny anything. Hence it is plain that **193** we adopt nonassertion also not as though things are in reality of such a kind as wholly to induce non-assertion, but as indicating that we now, at the time of uttering it, are in this condition regarding the problems now before us. It must also be borne in mind that what, as we say, we neither posit nor deny, is some one of the dogmatic statements made about what is nonapparent; for we yield to those things which move us emotionally and drive us compulsorily to assent.

CHAPTER XXI. OF THE EXPRESSIONS "PERHAPS," "POSSIBLY," AND "MAYBE"

The formulae "perhaps" and "perhaps not," and "pos- **194** sibly" and "possibly not," and "maybe" and "maybe not," we adopt in place of "perhaps it is and perhaps it is not," and "possibly it is and possibly it is not," and "maybe it is and maybe it is not," so that for the sake of conciseness we adopt the phrase "possibly not" instead of "possibly it is not," and "maybe not" instead of "maybe it is not," and "perhaps not" instead of "perhaps it is not." But here again we do not fight about phrases nor do we inquire whether the **195** phrases indicate realities, but we adopt them, as I said, in a loose sense. Still it is evident, as I think, that these expressions are indicative of nonassertion. Certainly the person who says "perhaps it is" is im-plicitly affirming also the seemingly contradictory phrase "perhaps it is not" by his refusal to make the positive assertion that "it is." And the same applies to all the other cases.

CHAPTER XXII. OF THE EXPRESSION "I SUSPEND JUDGMENT"

196 The phrase "I suspend judgment" we adopt in place of "I am unable to say which of the objects presented I ought to believe and which I ought to disbelieve," indicating that the objects appear to us equal as regards credibility and incredibility. As to whether they are equal we make no positive assertion; but what we state is what appears to us in regard to them at the time of observation. And the term "suspension" is derived from the fact of the mind being held up or "suspended" so that it neither affirms nor denies anything owing to the equipollence of the matters in question.

CHAPTER XXIII. OF THE EXPRESSION "I DETERMINE NOTHING"

197 Regarding the phrase "I detemine nothing" this is what we say. We hold that "to determine" is not simply to state a thing but to put forward something nonevident combined with assent. For in this sense, no doubt, it will be found that the skeptic determines nothing, not even the very proposition "I determine nothing"; for this is not a dogmatic assumption, that is to say assent to something nonevident, but an expression indicative of our own mental condition.

So whenever the skeptic says "I determine nothing," what he means is "I am now in such a state of mind as neither to affirm dogmatically nor deny any of the matters now in question." And this he says simply by way of announcing undogmatically what appears to himself regarding the matters presented, not making any confident declaration, but just explaining his own state of mind.

Chapter XXIV. Of the Expression "All Things are Undetermined"

Indetermination is a state of mind in which we neither **198** deny nor affirm any of the matters which are subjects of dogmatic inquiry, that is to say, nonevident. So whenever the skeptic says "All things are undetermined," he takes the word "are" in the sense of "appear to him," and by "all things" he means not existing things but such of the nonevident matters investigated by the dogmatists as he has examined, and by "undetermined" he means not superior in point of credibility or incredibility to things opposed, or in any way conflicting. And just as the man who says "(I) **199** walk about" is potentially saying "I walk about," so he who says "All are undetermined" conveys also, as we hold, the meaning "so far as relates to me," or "as appears to me," so that the statement amounts to this—"All the matters of dogmatic inquiry which I have examined appear to me to be such that no one of them is preferable to the one in conflict with it in respect of credibility or incredibility."

Chapter XXV. Of the Expression "All Things are Nonapprehensible"

200 We adopt a similar attitude when we say "All things are nonapprehensible." For we give a similar explanation of the word "all," and we similarly supply the words "to me," so that the meaning conveyed is this—"All the nonapparent matters of dogmatic inquiry which I have investigated appear to me nonapprehensible." And this is the utterance not of one who is positively asserting that the matters investigated by the dogmatists are really of such a nature as to be nonapprehensible, but of one who is announcing his own state of mind, "wherein," he says, "I conceive that up till now I myself have apprehended nothing owing to the equipollence of the opposites; and therefore also nothing that is brought forward to overthrow our position seems to me to have any bearing on what we announce."

Chapter XXVI. Of the Expressions "I am Nonapprehensive" and "I apprehend not"

201 Both the expressions "I am nonapprehensive" and "I apprehend not" are indicative of a personal state of mind, in which the skeptic, for the time being, avoids affirming or denying any nonevident matter of inquiry, as is obvious from what we have said above concerning the other expressions.

Chapter XXVII. Of the Phrase "To every Argument an Equal Argument is Opposed"

When we say "To every argument an equal argument **202** is opposed," we mean "to every argument" that has been investigated by us, and the word "argument" we use not in its simple sense, but of that which establishes a point dogmatically (that is to say with reference to what is nonevident) and establishes it by any method, and not necessarily by means of premises and a conclusion. We say "equal" with reference to credibility or incredibility, and we employ the word "opposed" in the general sense of "conflicting"; and we supply therewith in thought the phrase "as appears to me." So whenever I say "To **203** every argument an equal argument is opposed," what I am virtually saying is "To every argument investigated by me which establishes a point dogmatically, it seems to me there is opposed another argument, establishing a point dogmatically, which is equal to the first in respect of credibility and incredibility"; so that the utterance of the phrase is not a piece of dogmatism, but the announcement of a human state of mind which is apparent to the person experiencing it.

But some also utter the expression in the form **204** "To every argument an equal argument is to be opposed," intending to give the injunction "To every argument which establishes a point dogmatically let us oppose an argument which investigates dogmatically, equal to the former in respect of credibility and incredibility, and conflicting therewith"; for they mean their words to be addressed to the skeptic, although they use the infinitive "to be opposed" instead

205 of the imperative "let us oppose." And they address this injunction to the skeptic lest haply, through being misled by the dogmatist, he may give up the skeptic search, and through precipitancy miss the "quietude" approved by the skeptics, which they—as we said above—believe to be dependent on universal suspension of judgment.

CHAPTER XXVIII. SUPPLEMENTARY NOTES ON THE SKEPTIC EXPRESSIONS

206 In a preliminary outline it will be sufficient to have explained the expressions now set forth, especially since it is possible to explain the rest by deductions from the foregoing. For, in regard to all the skeptic expressions, we must grasp first the fact that we make no positive assertion respecting their absolute truth, since we say that they may possibly be confuted by themselves, seeing that they themselves are included in the things to which their doubt applies, just as aperient drugs do not merely eliminate the humors from the body, but also expel themselves along with

207 the humors. And we also say that we employ them not by way of authoritatively explaining the things with reference to which we adopt them, but without precision and, if you like, loosely; for it does not become the skeptic to wrangle over expressions, and besides it is to our advantage that even to these expressions no absolute significance would be ascribed, but one that is relative and relative to the skeptics. Besides this we must also remember that we do not **208** employ them universally about all things, but about those which are nonevident and are objects of dogmatic inquiry; and that we state what appears to us and do not make any positive declarations as to the real nature of external objects; for I think that, as a result of this, every sophism directed against a skeptic expression can be refuted.

And now that we have reviewed the idea or **209** purpose of skepticism and its divisions, and the criterion and the end, and the modes, too, of suspension, and have discussed the skeptic expressions, and have thus made clear the character of skepticism, our next task is, we suppose, to explain briefly the distinction which exists between it and the philosophic systems which lie next to it, in order that we may more clearly understand the "suspensive" way of thought. Let us begin with the Heracleitean philosophy.

CHAPTER XXIX. THAT THE SKEPTIC WAY OF THOUGHT DIFFERS FROM THE HERACLEITEAN PHILOSOPHY

Now that this latter differs from our way of thought **210** is plain at once; for Heracleitus* makes dogmatic statements about many nonevident things, whereas we, as has been said, do not. It is true that Aenesidemus and his followers used to say that the skeptic way

---

*[Fl. ca. 490 B.C. He declared that things are never the same but are continually changing.]

is a road leading up to the Heracleitean philosophy, since to hold that the same thing is the subject of opposite appearances is a preliminary to holding that it is the subject of opposite realities, and while the skeptics say that the same thing is the subject of opposite appearances, the Heracleiteans go on from this to assert their reality. But in reply to them we declare that the view about the same thing having opposite appearances is not a dogma of the skeptics but a fact which is experienced not by the skeptics alone but also by the rest of philosophers and by all mankind; for certainly

211 no one would venture to say that honey does not taste sweet to people in sound health or that it does not taste bitter to those suffering from jaundice; so that the Heracleiteans start from the general preconception of mankind, just as we also do and probably all the other philosophies. Consequently, if they had derived their theory that the same thing is the subject of opposite realities from one of the skeptic formulae, such as "All things are nonapprehensible," or "I determine nothing," or some similar expression, probably they would have reached the conclusion they assert; but since their starting points are impressions experienced not by us only but by all the other philosophers and by ordinary people, why should anyone declare that our way of thought is a road to the Heracleitean philosophy any more than any of the other philosophies or even than the ordinary view, since we all make use of the same common material?*

---

*I.e., general human experience and observation, derived from sense impressions.

Rather it is the case that the skeptic way, so **212** far from being an aid to the knowledge of the Heracleitean philosophy, is actually an obstacle thereto, seeing that the skeptic decries all the dogmatic statements of Heracleitus as rash utterances, contradicting his "Ecpyrosis,"* and contradicting his view that the same thing is the subject of opposite realities, and in respect of every dogma of Heracleitus scoffing at his dogmatic precipitancy, and constantly repeating, as I said before, his own "I apprehend not" and "I determine nothing," which are in conflict with the Heracleiteans. Now it is absurd to say that a conflicting way is a road to the system with which it is in conflict; therefore it is absurd to say that the skeptic way is a road leading to the Heracleitean philosophy.

CHAPTER XXX. WHEREIN THE SKEPTIC WAY DIFFERS FROM THE DEMOCRITEAN PHILOSOPHY

But it is also said that the Democritean† philosophy **213** has something in common with skepticism, since it seems to use the same material as we; for from the fact that honey appears sweet to some and bitter to others, Democritus, as they say, infers that it really is neither sweet nor bitter, and pronounces in consequence the formula "Not more," which is a skeptic

---

*I.e., "world-conflagration," by which all things are resolved into the primal fire.

†[Democritus (ca. 460-370 B.C.), who developed the atomic theory of Leucippus, held that the world is made up of "the full" (solid, indivisible molecules of matter) and "the empty" (space or void)].

214 formula. The skeptics, however, and the school of Democritus employ the expression "Not more" in different ways; for while they use it to express the unreality of either alternative, we express by it our ignorance as to whether both or neither of the appearances is real. So that in this respect also we differ, and our difference becomes specially evident when Democritus says "But in verity atoms and void" (for he says "In verity" in place of "In truth"); and that he differs from us when he says that the atoms and the void are in truth subsistent, although he starts out from the incongruity of appearances, it is superfluous, I think, to state.

CHAPTER XXXI. WHEREIN SKEPTICISM DIFFERS FROM CYRENAICISM

215 Some assert that the Cyrenaic doctrine is identical with skepticism since it too affirms that only mental states are apprehended. But it differs from skepticism inasmuch as it says that the end is pleasure and the smooth motion of the flesh, whereas we say it is "quietude," which is the opposite of their end; for whether pleasure be present or not present the man who positively affirms pleasure to be the end undergoes perturbations, as I have argued in my chapter "Of the End." Further, whereas we suspend judgment, so far as regards the essence of external objects, the Cyrenaics declare that those objects possess a real nature which is inapprehensible.

Chapter XXXII. Wherein Skepticism Differs from the Protagorean Doctrine

Protagoras* also holds that "Man is the measure of **216** all things, of existing things that they exist, and of nonexisting things that they exist not"; and by "measure" he means the criterion, and by "things" the objects, so that he is virtually asserting that "Man is the criterion of all objects, of those which exist that they exist, and of those which exist not that they exist not." And consequently he posits only what appears to each individual, and thus he introduces relativity. And for this reason he seems also to have **217** something in common with the Pyrrhoneans. Yet he differs from them, and we shall perceive the difference when we have adequately explained the views of Protagoras.

What he states then is this—that matter is in flux, and as it flows additions are made continuously in the place of the effluxions, and the senses are transformed and altered according to the times of life and to all the other conditions of the bodies. He says also that the "reasons" of all the appearances **218** subsist in matter, so that matter, so far as depends on itself, is capable of being all those things which appear to all. And men, he says, apprehend different things at different times owing to their differing dispositions; for he who is in a natural state apprehends those things subsisting in matter which are able to

---

*[Ca. 485–410 B.C. Friend of the Athenian statesman Pericles and known as the first of the sophists.]

appear to those in a natural state, and those who are in a nonnatural state the things which can appear

219 to those in a nonnatural state. Moreover, precisely the same account applies to the variations due to age, and to the sleeping or waking state, and to each several kind of condition. Thus, according to him, man becomes the criterion of real existences; for all things that appear to men also exist, and things that appear to no man have no existence either.

We see, then, that he dogmatizes about the fluidity of matter and also about the subsistence therein of the "reasons" of all appearances, these being nonevident matters about which we suspend judgment.

Chapter XXXIII. Wherein Skepticism Differs from the Academic Philosophy

220 Some indeed say that the Academic philosophy is identical with skepticism; consequently it shall be our next task to discuss this statement.

According to most people there have been three Academies—the first and most ancient that of Plato and his school, the second or middle Academy that of Arcesilaus, the pupil of Polemo, and his school, the third or new Academy that of the school of Carneades and Cleitomachus. Some, however, add as a fourth that of the school of Philo and Charmidas; and some even count the school of Antiochus as

221 a fifth. Beginning, then, with the old Academy let us consider how the philosophies mentioned differ from ours.

Plato has been described by some as "dogmatic," by others as "dubitative," and by others again as partly dogmatic and partly dubitative. For in his exercitatory discourses, where Socrates is introduced either as talking playfully with his auditors or as arguing against sophists, he shows, they say, an exercitatory and dubitative character; but a dogmatic character when he is speaking seriously by the mouth either of Socrates or of Timaeus or of some similar personage. Now as regards those who describe him as a dog- **222** matist, or as partly dogmatic and partly dubitative, it would be superfluous to say anything now; for they themselves acknowledge his difference from us. But the question whether Plato is a genuine skeptic is one which we discuss more fully in our "Commentaries"*; but now, in opposition to Menodotus† and Aenesidemus (these being the chief champions of this view), we declare in brief that when Plato makes statements about ideas or about the reality of providence or about the virtuous life being preferable to the vicious, he is dogmatizing if he is assenting to these as actual truths, while if he is accepting them as more probable than not, since thereby he gives a preference to one thing over another in point of probability or improbability, he throws off the character of a skeptic; for that such an attitude is foreign to us is quite plain from what has been said above.

And if Plato does really utter some statements **223**

---

*I.e., the five books *Against the Dogmatists.*

†[Fl. ca. A.D. 120. Leader of the empirical school of medicine and often referred to in the later medical writings of Galen.]

in a skeptical way when he is, as they say, "exercising," that will not make him a skeptic; for the man that dogmatizes about a single thing, or ever prefers one impression to another in point of credibility or incredibility, or makes any assertion about any non-evident object, assumes the dogmatic character, as

224 Timon* also shows by his remarks about Xenophanes. For after praising him repeatedly, so that he even dedicated to him his *Satires,* he represented him as uttering this lamentation—

> Would that I too had attained a mind compacted of
>   wisdom,
> Both ways casting my eyes; but the treacherous
>   pathway deceived me,
> Old that I was, and as yet unversed in the doubts
>   of the skeptic.
> For in whatever direction I turned my mind in its
>   questing
> All was resolved into One and the Same; All ever-
>   existing
> Into one selfsame nature returning shaped itself all ways.

So on this account he also calls him "semi-vain," and not perfectly free from vanity, where he says—

> Xenophanes semi-vain, derider of Homer's deceptions,
> Framed him a god far other than man, self-equal
>   in all ways
> Safe from shaking or scathe, surpassing thought in
>   his thinking.

---

*[Ca. 320 230 B.C. The most famous of his extant writings are the *Silloi* (i.e., mock-poetry) ridiculing all dogmatic philosophers.]

He called him "semi-vain" as being in some degree free from vanity, and "derider of Homer's deceptions" because he censured the deceit mentioned in Homer. Xenophanes, contrary to the preconceptions of all **225** other men, asserted dogmatically that the All is one, and that God is consubstantial with all things, and is of spherical form and passionless and unchangeable and rational; and from this it is easy to show how Xenophanes differs from us. However, it is plain from what has been said that even if Plato evinces doubt about some matters, yet he cannot be a skeptic inasmuch as he shows himself at times either making assertions about the reality of nonevident objects or preferring one nonevident thing to another in point of credibility.

The adherents of the new Academy, although **226** they affirm that all things are nonapprehensible, yet differ from the skeptics even, as seems probable, in respect of this very statement that all things are nonapprehensible (for they affirm this positively, whereas the skeptic regards it as possible that some things may be apprehended); but they differ from us quite plainly in their judgment of things good and evil. For the Academicians do not describe a thing as good or evil in the way we do; for they do so with the conviction that it is more probable that what they call good is really good rather than the opposite, and so too in the case of evil, whereas when we describe a thing as good or evil we do not add it as our opinion that what we assert is probable, but simply conform to life undogmatically that we may

227   not be precluded from activity. And as regards sense impressions, we say that they are equal in respect of probability and improbability, so far as their essence is concerned, whereas they assert that some impressions are probable, others improbable.

And respecting the probable impressions they make distinctions: some they regard as just simply probable, others as probable and tested, others as probable, tested, and "irreversible." For example, when a rope is lying coiled up in a dark room, to one who enters hurriedly it presents the simply

228   "probable" appearance of being a serpent; but to the man who has looked carefully round and has investigated the conditions—such as its immobility and its color, and each of its other peculiarities—it appears as a rope, in accordance with an impression that is probable and tested. And the impression that is also "irreversible" or incontrovertible is of this kind. When Alcestis had died, Heracles, it is said, brought her up again from Hades and showed her to Admetus, who received an impression of Alcestis that was probable and tested; since, however, he knew that she was dead his mind recoiled from its assent

229   and reverted to unbelief. So then the philosophers of the new Academy prefer the probable and tested impression to the simply probable, and to both of these the impression that is probable and tested and irreversible.

And although both the Academics and the skeptics say that they believe some things, yet here too the difference between the two philosophies is

quite plain. For the word "believe" has different mean- **230**
ings: it means not to resist but simply to follow without
any strong impulse or inclination, as the boy is said
to believe his tutor; but sometimes it means to assent
to a thing of deliberate choice and with a kind of
sympathy due to strong desire, as when the incon-
tinent man believes him who approves of an extrava-
gant mode of life. Since, therefore, Carneades and
Cleitomachus declare that a strong inclination ac-
companies their credence and the credibility of the
object, while we say that our belief is a matter of
simple yielding without any consent, here too there
must be a difference between us and them.

Furthermore, as regards the end (or aim of life) **231**
we differ from the new Academy; for whereas the
men who profess to conform to its doctrine use
probability as the guide of life, we live in an undogmatic way by following the laws, customs, and
natural affections. And we might say still more about
this distinction had it not been that we are aiming
at conciseness.

Arcesilaus, however, who was, as we said, the **232**
president and founder of the middle Academy, certainly seems to me to have shared the doctrines of
Pyrrho, so that his way of thought is almost identical
with ours. For we do not find him making any
assertion about the reality or unreality of anything,
nor does he prefer any one thing to another in point
of probability or improbability, but suspends judgment about all. He also says that the end is suspension—which is accompanied, as we have said, by

233   "quietude." He declares, too, that suspension regarding particular objects is good, but assent regarding particulars bad. Only one might say that whereas we make these statements not positively but in accordance with what appears to us, he makes them as statements of real facts, so that he asserts that suspension in itself really is good and assent bad.

234   And if one ought to credit also what is said about him, he appeared at the first glance, they say, to be a Pyrrhonean, but in reality he was a dogmatist; and because he used to test his companions by means of dubitation to see if they were fitted by nature for the reception of the Platonic dogmas, he was thought to be a dubitive philosopher, but he actually passed on to such of his companions as were naturally gifted the dogmas of Plato. And this was why Ariston* described him as "Plato the head of him, Pyrrho the tail, in the midst Diodorus"†; because he employed the dialectic of Diodorus, although he was actually a Platonist.

235   Philo asserts that objects are inapprehensible so far as concerns the Stoic criterion, that is to say "apprehensive impression," but are apprehensible so far as concerns the real nature of the objects themselves. Moreover, Antiochus‡ actually transferred the Stoa to the Academy, so that it was even said of him that "In the Academy he teaches the Stoic phi-

---

*[Fl. 250 B.C. Pupil of Zeno, founder of the Stoic school, and the most influential philosopher of his day at Athens.]

†[Fl. ca. 300 B.C. Teacher of Zeno and Arcesilaus.]

‡[Philo of Larissa (d. ca. 80 B.C.) and Antiochus (d. 69 B.C.) succeeded Carneades as head of the new Academy.]

losophy"; for he tried to show that the dogmas of the Stoics are already present in Plato. So that it is quite plain how the skeptic "way" differs from what is called the fourth Academy and the fifth.

CHAPTER XXXIV. WHETHER MEDICAL EMPIRICISM IS THE SAME AS SKEPTICISM

Since some allege that the skeptic philosophy is identical with the empiricism of the medical sect,*it **236** must be recognized that inasmuch as that empiricism positively affirms the inapprehensibility of what is nonevident it is not identical with skepticism nor would it be consistent in a skeptic to embrace that doctrine. He could more easily, in my opinion, adopt the so-called "method"; for it alone of the medical **237** systems appears to avoid rash treatment of things nonevident by arbitrary assertions as to their apprehensibility or nonapprehensibility, and following appearances derives from them what seems beneficial, in accordance with the practice of the skeptics. For we stated above that the common life, in which the skeptic also shares, is fourfold, one part depending on the directing force of nature, another on the compulsion of the affections, another on the tradition of laws and customs, and another on the training of the arts. So then, just as the skeptic, in virtue **238**

---

*The later schools of medicine were three: (1) the dogmatic or logical, which theorized about the "nonevident" causes of health and disease; (2) the empiric, which regarded such causes as indiscoverable and confined itself to observation of evident facts; (3) the methodic, which adopted an intermediate position, refusing either to affirm or deny "nonevident" causes.

of the compulsion of the affections, is guided by thirst to drink and by hunger to food, and in like manner to other such objects, in the same way the methodical physician is guided by the pathological affections to the corresponding remedies—by contraction to dilatation, as when one seeks refuge in heat from the contraction due to the application of cold, or by fluxion to the stoppage of it, as when persons in a hot bath, dripping with perspiration and in a relaxed condition, seek to put a stop to it and for this reason rush off into the cool air. It is plain, too, that conditions which are naturally alien compel us to take measures for their removal, seeing that even the dog when it is pricked by a thorn proceeds

239 to remove it. And in short—to avoid exceeding the limits proper to an outline of this kind by a detailed enumeration—I suppose that all the facts described by the methodic school can be classed as instances of the compulsion of the affections, whether natural or against nature.

Besides, the use of terms in an undogmatic and
240 indeterminate sense is common to both systems. For just as the skeptic uses the expressions "I determine nothing" and "I apprehend nothing," as we have said, in an undogmatic sense, even so the methodic speaks of "generality" and "pervade" and the like in a non-committal way. So also he employs the term "indication" in an undogmatic sense to denote the guidance derived from the apparent affections, or symptoms, both natural and contra-natural, for the discovery of the seemingly appropriate remedies—

as, in fact, I mentioned in regard to hunger and thirst and the other affections. Consequently, judging from **241** these and similar indications, we should say that the methodic school of medicine has some affinity with skepticism; and, when viewed not simply by itself, but in comparison with the other medical schools, it has more affinity than they.

And now that we have said thus much concerning the schools which seem to stand nearest to that of the skeptics, we here bring to a conclusion both our general account of skepticism and the first book of our "Outlines."

BOOK II

Chapter I. Can the Skeptic investigate the Statements of the Dogmatists?

1 Since we have undertaken this inquiry in criticism of the dogmatists, let us review briefly and in outline the several divisions of so-called philosophy, when we have first made reply to those who keep constantly repeating that the skeptic is incapable of either investigating or in any way cognizing the objects about **2** which they dogmatize. For they* maintain that the skeptic either apprehends or does not apprehend the statements made by the dogmatists; if, then, he apprehends, how can he be perplexed about things which he has, as he says, apprehended? Whereas if he apprehends not, then neither does he know how to discuss matters which he has not apprehended. For **3** just as he who is ignorant, for instance, of the arguments known as "How far reduced" or "By two hypotheses,"† is unable also to say anything about them, so the man who does not know each of the state-

---

*I.e., the Stoics and Epicureans.

†The hypothetical syllogism "by two hypotheses" has its major premise in double form; e.g., "If A is, B is, and if A is not, B is; but A either is or is not; therefore B is."

ments made by the dogmatists is unable to criticize them concerning matters of which he has no knowledge. Thus the skeptic is wholly incapable of investigating the statements made by the dogmatists.

Now let those who speak thus make answer and 4 tell us in what sense they are now using the term "apprehend," whether simply of mental conception without the further affirmation of the reality of the objects under discussion, or with the further assumption of the reality of the objects discussed. For if they say that "to apprehend" means, in their argument, to assent to an "apprehensive impression,"* the apprehensive impression being derived from a real object and being an imprint or stamp upon the mind corresponding to the actual object, such as would not result from what is unreal, then probably not even they themselves will wish to allow their inability to investigate things which, in this sense, they have not apprehended. Thus, for example, when the Stoic criti- 5 cizes the statement of the Epicurean that "Being is divided," or that "God does not foreknow events in the universe," or that "Pleasure is Good," has he apprehended or has he not apprehended? If he has apprehended these dogmas, by asserting their real truth he entirely overthrows the Porch; while if he has not

---

*[In Stoic epistemology, this term refers to an impression made on the soul by existent things which are perceived through the senses. Succinctly, knowledge is the agreement of one's mental conceptions with reality.] The argument is, in brief, that the Stoic cannot consistently criticize the Epicurean unless he allows that his "apprehensive impression" of their dogmas is an impression of things which have no basis in reality, and this contradicts the Stoic definition of "apprehensive impression."

apprehended them, he is unable to say anything against them.

6 And we must use a like argument against those who issue from any of the other sects, whenever they desire to make any critical investigation of the tenets of those who differ from them in doctrine. Consequently they are debarred from indulging in any criticism of one another. Or rather—to avoid talking nonsense—practically the whole of dogmatism will be confounded and the skeptic philosophy will be firmly established once it is granted that it is impossible to inquire regarding an object which is not,

7 in this sense, apprehended. For he who makes a dogmatic statement about a nonevident object will declare that he is making it either after having apprehended or after not having apprehended it. But if he has not apprehended it he will not gain credence; while if he has apprehended it, he will say that he has apprehended the object directly and through itself and owing to the clear impression it has made on him, or else by means of some kind of search and

8 inquiry. But if he shall say that the nonevident object has impressed him and has been apprehended through itself, immediately and clearly, in this case the object would not be nonevident but apparent to all men equally, an acknowledged and uncontroverted fact. But about every single object that is nonevident there exists among them endless controversy; so that the dogmatist who makes positive assertions about the reality of a nonevident object cannot have apprehended it because of its having made on him a direct

and clear impression. If, on the other hand, his apprehension is the result of search, how was he in **9** a position to make inquiry before he had accurately apprehended the object, without violating our present assumption? For since the inquiry necessitates as a preliminary the existence of an accurate apprehension of that which is to be the subject of inquiry, while the apprehension of the subject of inquiry demands, in its turn, the previous existence of a complete inquiry into that subject, owing to this circular process of reasoning it becomes impossible for them either to inquire concerning things nonevident or to dogmatize; for if some of them wish to make apprehension their starting point we force them to grant that the object must be investigated before it is apprehended, while if they start from inquiry we make them admit that before inquiring they must apprehend the object of the inquiry, so that for these reasons they can neither apprehend any nonevident object nor make positive statements about them. From this there will follow automatically, as I think, the demolition of the dogmatic sophistry and the establishment of the suspensive philosophy.

If, however, they say that it is not this kind of **10** apprehension that ought, in their view, to precede inquiry, but simply mental conception, then it is no longer impossible for those who suspend judgment to inquire about the reality of things nonevident. For the skeptic is not, I suppose, prohibited from mental conception which arises through the reason itself as a result of passive impressions and clear appearances and does not at all involve the reality of the objects conceived; for we conceive, as they say, not only of real things but also of unreal. Hence both while inquiring and while conceiving, the suspensive person continues in the skeptical state of mind. For, as has been shown, he assents to what he experiences by way of subjective impression, according as that impression appears to him. But consider whether, even

11 in this case, the dogmatists are not precluded from inquiry. For to continue the investigation of problems

27 is not inconsistent in those who confess their ignorance of their real nature, but only in those who believe they have an exact knowledge of them; since for the latter the inquiry has already, as they suppose, reached its goal, whereas for the former the ground on which all inquiry is based—namely, the belief that they have not found the truth—still subsists.

12 Thus we have to inquire briefly, on the present occasion, concerning each several division of philosophy so called. And since there exists much dispute amongst the dogmatists regarding the divisions of philosophy—some saying there is one division, some two, some three—and it would not now be convenient to discuss the question at length, we will explain fairly and impartially the view of those who seem to have treated it most fully, and take their view as the subject of our discourse.

Chapter II. The Starting point for Criticism of the Dogmatists

The Stoics, then, and several others, say that there **13** are three divisions of philosophy, namely, logic, physics, and ethics; and they begin their teaching with logic, although the question of the right starting point is also a matter of much controversy. So we shall follow them in an undogmatic way; and since the subject matter of all three divisions requires testing and a criterion, and the doctrine of the criterion seems to be included in the division of logic, we shall begin with the doctrine of the criterion and the division of logic.

Chapter III. Of the Criterion

But first we must notice that the word "criterion" **14** is used both of that by which, as they say, we judge of reality and nonreality, and of that which we use as the guide of life; and our present task is to discuss the so-called criterion of truth, since we have already dealt with the criterion in its other sense in our discourse "On Skepticism."

The criterion, then, with which our argument **15** is concerned, has three several meanings—the general, the special, and the most special. In the "general" sense it is used of every standard of apprehension, and in this sense we speak even of physical organs, such as sight, as criteria. In the "special" sense it includes every technical standard of apprehension, such as the rule and the compass. In the "most special" sense it includes every technical standard of apprehension of a nonevident object; but in this application ordinary standards* are not regarded as criteria but only logical standards and those which the dogmatists 16 employ for the judging of truth. We propose, therefore, in the first place to discuss the logical criterion. But the logical criterion also may be used in three senses—of the agent, or the instrument, or the "according to what"; the agent, for instance, may be a man, the instrument either sense perception or intelligence, and the "according to what" the application of the impression "according to" which the man proceeds to judge by means of one of the aforesaid instruments.

17   It was appropriate, I consider, to make these prefatory observations so that we may realize what is the exact object of our discourse; and it remains for us to proceed to our counterstatement aimed against those who rashly assert that they have apprehended the criterion of truth, and we will begin with the dispute which exists about this question.

CHAPTER IV. DOES A CRITERION OF TRUTH REALLY EXIST?

18   Of those, then, who have treated of the criterion some have declared that a criterion exists—the Stoics, for example, and certain others—while by some its exis-

---

*I.e., standards of weight and measure (e.g., pound, pint, yard).

tence is denied, as by the Corinthian Xeniades,* amongst others, and by Xenophanes of Colophon,† who says—"Over all things opinion bears sway"; while we have adopted suspension of judgment as to **6** whether it does or does not exist. This dispute, then, **19** they will declare to be either capable or incapable of decision; and if they shall say it is incapable of decision they will be granting on the spot the propriety of suspension of judgment, while if they say it admits of decision, let them tell us whereby it is to be decided, since we have no accepted criterion, and do not even know, but are still inquiring, whether any criterion exists. Besides, in order to decide the dispute which **20** has arisen about the criterion, we must possess an accepted criterion by which we shall be able to judge the dispute; and in order to possess an accepted criterion, the dispute about the criterion must first be decided. And when the argument thus reduces itself to a form of circular reasoning, the discovery of the criterion becomes impracticable, since we do not allow them to adopt a criterion by assumption, while if they offer to judge the criterion by a criterion we force them to a regress *ad infinitum.* And furthermore, since demonstration requires a demonstrated criterion, while the criterion requires an approved demonstration, they are forced into circular reasoning.

---

*[A philosopher who lived before Democritus (ca. 460–370 B.C.).]

†[Ca. 560–478 B.C. Philosopher and poet who denied that the Olympian gods have a human shape or understanding. There is but one deity who sways the universe through thought.]

21   We suppose, then, that this is sufficient to expose the rashness of the dogmatists in respect of their doctrine of the criterion; but in order to enable us to confute them in detail, it will not be out of place to dwell at length upon this topic. We do not, however, desire to oppose their opinions about the criterion severally, one by one—for their controversy is endless, and to do so would necessarily involve us as well in a confused discussion,—but inasmuch as the criterion in question is threefold (the agent, the instrument, and the "according to what"), we shall discuss each of these in turn and establish the nonapprehensibility of each, since in this way our exposition will be at once both methodical and complete. Let us begin with the agent; for the perplexity which attaches to this seems somehow to involve the rest as well.

CHAPTER V. OF THE CRITERION "BY WHOM," OR AGENT

22 Now "man" (if he is "the agent") seems to me, so far as regards the statements made by the dogmatists, to be not only nonapprehensible but also inconceivable. At least we hear the Platonic Socrates expressly confessing that he does not know whether he is a man or something else. And when they wish to establish the concept of "man" they disagree in the first place, and in the second place they speak unintelligibly.

23   Thus Democritus declares that "Man is that

which we all know." Then, so far as his opinion goes, we shall not know Man, since we also know a dog, and consequently Dog too will be Man. And some men we do not know, therefore they will not be men. Or rather, if we are to judge by this concept, no one will be a man; for since Democritus says that Man must be known by all, and all men know no one man, no one, according to him, will be a man. **24** And it is evident from the relevance of this criticism that we are not now arguing sophistically. For this thinker proceeds to say that "Only the atoms and the void truly exist," and these he says "form the substrate not only of animals but of all compound substances," so that, so far as depends on these, we shall not form a concept of the particular essence of "man," seeing that they are common to all things. But besides these there is no existing substrate; so that we shall possess no means whereby we shall be able to distinguish man from the other animals and form a precise conception of him.

Again, Epicurus says that Man is "This sort of **25** a shape combined with vitality."* According to him, then, since Man is shown by pointing out, he that is not pointed out is not a man, and if anyone points out a female, the male will not be Man, while if he points out a male the female will not be Man. And we shall also draw the same inferences from

---

*Epicurus taught that truth is given by sense perception: the percept is the real "thing in itself"; hence we have no general concepts which can be logically "defined" but only particular phenomena which are "indicated" or pointed out as "such and such, look you."

the difference in the circumstances which we learn from the fourth mode of suspension.

Others used to assert that "Man is a rational mortal animal, receptive of intelligence and science." Now since it is shown by the first mode of suspension that no animal is irrational but all are receptive of intelligence and science, so far as their statements go, we shall be unable to perceive what they mean. And the attributes contained in this definition are used either in an "actual," or full, or in a potential sense; if in a full sense, he that has not already acquired complete science and is not rationally perfect and in the very act of dying—for this is to be mortal in the full sense of the word—is not a man. And if the sense is to be potential, then he will not be a man who possesses reason in perfection or who has acquired intelligence and science; but this conclusion is even more absurd than the former.

28 In this way, then, the concept of Man is shown to be one which it is impossible to frame. For when Plato declares that "Man is a featherless two-footed animal with broad nails, receptive of political science," not even he himself claims to affirm this positively; for if Man is one of the class of things which, as he puts it, come into being but never possess absolute being, and if it is impossible, in his view, to make a positive declaration about things which never really exist, then even Plato will not claim to be taken as putting forward this definition positively, but rather as making, in his usual way, a probable statement.

29 But even if we should grant, by way of concession,

that Man can be conceived, yet he will be found to be nonapprehensible. For he is compounded of soul and body, and neither body nor soul perchance is apprehended; so that Man is not apprehended. Now that body is not apprehended is easily shown **30** thus: the attributes of an object are different from the object whereof they are attributes. So when color or any similar quality is perceived by us, what we perceive is probably the attributes of the body but not the body itself. Certainly the body, they say, exists in three dimensions; we ought therefore to apprehend its length and breadth and depth in order to apprehend the body. For if we perceived depth we should also discern silver pieces under their coating of gold. Therefore we do not apprehend the body either.

But, not to dwell on the controversy about the **31** body, Man is also found to be nonapprehensible owing to the fact that his soul is nonapprehensible. That it is nonapprehensible is plain from this: of those who have treated of the soul—so that we may avoid dwelling on the long and endless controversy—some have asserted, as did Dicaearchus the Messenian,* that the soul has no existence, others that it has existence, and others have suspended judgment. If, then, the dogmatists shall maintain that this dispute **32** is incapable of decision, they will be admitting thereby the nonapprehensibility of the soul, while if they say it is capable of decision, let them tell us by what means they will decide it. For they cannot say "by

---

*A student of Aristotle.

sense perception," since the soul is said by them to be an object of intelligence; and if they shall say "by the intellect," we will say that inasmuch as the intellect is the least evident part of the soul—as is shown by those who agree about the real existence of the

33 soul, though differing about the intellect,—if they propose to apprehend the soul and to decide the dispute about it by means of the intellect, they will be proposing to decide and establish the less questionable matter by the more questionable, which is absurd. Thus, neither by the intellect will the dispute about the soul be decided; therefore there is no means to decide it. And this being so, it is nonapprehensible; and, in consequence, Man too will not be apprehended.

34 But even supposing we grant that Man is apprehended, it would not, probably, be possible to show that objects ought to be judged by him. For he who asserts that objects ought to be judged by Man will be asserting this either without proof or with proof. Not with proof; for the proof must be true and tested, and therefore tested by some standard. Since, then, we are unable to make an agreed statement as to the standard by which the proof itself can be tested (for we are still inquiring about the criterion "By whom"), we shall be unable to pronounce judgment on the proof, and therefore also to prove the criterion,

35 which is the subject of discussion. And if it shall be asserted without proof that objects ought to be judged by Man, the assertion will be disbelieved, so that we shall be unable to affirm positively that the criterion

"By whom" (or agent) is Man. Moreover, who is to be the judge that the criterion or the agent is Man? For if they assert this without a judgment (or criterion) they will surely not be believed. Yet if they say that **36** a man is to be the judge, that will be assuming the point at issue; while if they make another animal the judge, in what way do they come to adopt that animal for the purpose of judging whether Man is the criterion? If they do so without a judgment, it will not be believed, and if with a judgment, it in turn needs to be judged by something. If, then, it is judged by itself, the same absurdity remains (for the object of inquiry will be judged by the object of inquiry); and if by Man, circular reasoning is introduced; and if by some judge other than these two, we shall once again in his case demand the criterion "By whom," and so on *ad infinitum*. Consequently we shall not be in a position to declare that objects ought to be judged by Man.

But let it be granted and established that objects **37** ought to be judged by Man. Then, since there exists great difference amongst men, let the dogmatists first agree together that this is the particular man to whom we must attend, and then, and only then, let them bid us also to yield him our assent. But if they are going to dispute about this "long as the waters flow on and the tall trees cease not to burgeon" (to quote the familiar saying),* how can they urge us to assent rashly to anyone? For if they declare that we must **38**

---

*From the inscription on the tomb of Midas quoted in Plato, *Phaedrus* 264b.

believe the sage, we shall ask them "What sage?" Is it the sage of Epicurus or of the Stoics, the Cyrenaic sage or the Cynic? For they will be unable to return a unanimous answer.

39 And if anyone shall demand that we should desist from our inquiry about the sage and simply believe the man who is more sagacious than all others, then, in the first place, they will dispute as to who is more sagacious than the rest, and in the next place, even if it be granted that it can be unanimously agreed who the man is who is more sagacious than those of the present and the past, even so this man will **40** not deserve credence. For inasmuch as sagacity is liable to a great, indeed almost incalculable, advance of decline in intensity, we assert that it is possible for another man to arise who is more sagacious than this man who, we say, is more sagacious than those of the past and present. So, then, just as we are requested to believe the man who is now said to be wiser than those of the present and the past because of his sagacity, so it is still more proper to believe his successor in the future who will be more sagacious than he. And when that successor has arisen, then it is right to expect that yet another will arise more **41** sagacious than he, and so on *ad infinitum*. Nor is it evident whether all these men will agree with one another or contradict one another. And consequently, even when one of them is acknowledged to be more sagacious than those of the past and present, seeing that we are unable to affirm positively that no man will be more clever than he (this being nonevident), we shall always have to wait for the judgment of the more sagacious man of the future, and never give our assent to this superior person.

And even should we grant, by way of concession, **42** that no one either is, was, or will be more sagacious than our hypothetical sage, not even so is it proper to believe him. For since it is the sagacious above all who, in the construction of their doctrines, love to champion unsound doctrines and to make them appear sound and true, whenever this sharp-witted person makes a statement we shall not know whether he is stating the matter as it really is, or whether he is defending as true what is really false and persuading us to think of it as something true, on the gound that he is more sagacious than all other men and therefore incapable of being refuted by us. So not even to this man will we assent, as one who judges matters truly, since, though we suppose it possible that he speaks the truth, we also suppose that owing to his excessive cleverness he makes his statements with the object of defending false propositions as true. Consequently, in the judgment of propositions we ought not to believe even the man who is thought to be the most clever of all.

And if anyone shall say that we ought to attend **43** to the consensus of the majority, we shall reply that this is idle. For, in the first place, truth is a rare thing, and on this account it is possible for one man to be wiser than the majority. And, next, the opponents of any criterion are more numerous than those who agree about it; for those who admit any kind of criterion different from that which seems to some to be generally agreed upon oppose this latter, and they

44 are much more numerous than those who agree about it. And besides all this, those who agree are either in diverse dispositions or in one and the same. Now they certainly are not in diverse dispositions so far as regards the matter under discussion; else how could they have made identical statements about it? And if they are in one disposition, inasmuch as both the one man who makes a different statement is in one disposition and all these who agree together are also in one, so far as regards the dispositions in which we find ourselves, no difference is found even on the ground of numbers. Consequently we ought not to

45 pay heed to the many more than to the one; besides the further fact that—as we pointed out in "The Fourth Mode of Skepticism"—the difference in judgments that is based on numbers is nonapprehensible, since individual men are innumerable and we are incapable of investigating and expounding the judgments of all of them—what it is the majority of all mankind affirm and what the minority. Thus, on this showing also, the preference given to men's judgments on the ground of their numbers is absurd.

46 But if we are not even to give heed to numbers, we shall not find anyone by whom objects are to be judged, in spite of our having granted so much by way of concession. Therefore, on all these grounds, the criterion "By whom" objects are to be judged is found to be nonapprehensible.

47 And seeing that the other criteria are included

in this one, since each of them is either a part of an affection or an activity of Man, our next task might perhaps have been to proceed in our discussion to one of the subjects which follows next in order, supposing that those criteria also have been sufficiently dealt with in what we have now said; yet in order that we may not seem to be shirking the specific counterstatement proper to each case, we will exceed our brief and deal with them also shortly. And we shall discuss first the criterion "By means of which" (or instrument) as it is called.

CHAPTER VI. OF THE CRITERION "BY MEANS OF WHICH" (OR INSTRUMENT)

Concerning this criterion the controversy which exists **48** amongst the dogmatists is fierce and, one may say, unending. We, however,—with a view here also to a systematic treatment,—maintain that inasmuch as Man is, according to them, the criterion "By whom" matters are judged, and Man (as they also themselves agree) can have no other instrument by means of which he will be able to judge except sense and intellect, then if we shall show that he is unable to judge by means of either sense alone or intellect alone or both conjoined, we shall have given a concise answer to all the individual opinions; for they can all, as it seems, be referred to these three rival theories. Let us begin with the senses.

Since, then, some* assert that the senses have **49**

___
*[E.g., Heracleitus and Democritus.]

"empty" impressions (none of the objects they seem to apprehend having any real existence), and others* say that all the objects by which they suppose them to be moved are really existent, and others again† say that some of the objects are real, some unreal, we shall not know whom we should assent to. For we shall not decide the controversy by sense perception, since it is regarding this that we are making our inquiry whether it is illusory or apprehends truly, nor yet by anything else, seeing that there does not even exist any other criterion "by means of which" one ought to judge, according to the present hypoth-

50 esis. So then the question whether the senses have illusory affections or apprehend some real object will be incapable of either decision or apprehension; and there follows the corollary, that we must not attend to sensation alone in our judgment of matters, since regarding it we cannot so much as affirm that it apprehends anything at all.

51 But let it be granted, by way of concession, that the senses are apprehensive; yet, even so they will not be found any the less unreliable for judging the external real objects. For certainly the senses are affected in diverse ways by external objects—taste, for instance, perceives the same honey now as bitter and now as sweet; and vision pronounces the same

52 color now blood-red and now white. Nay, even smell is not consistent with itself; for certainly the sufferer from headache declares myrrh to be unpleasant, while

---

*Epicurus and Protagoras.
†Peripatetics, Stoics, and Academics.

one who does not so suffer calls it pleasant. And those who are possessed or in a frenzy fancy they hear persons conversing with them whom we do not hear. And the same water seems to those in a fever to be unpleasant because of its excessive heat, but to all others tepid. Whether, then, one is to call all **53** the appearances true, or some true and some false, or all false, it is impossible to say since we possess no agreed criterion whereby we shall judge the question we are proposing to decide, nor are we even provided with a proof that is true and approved, because we are still in search of the criterion of truth "by means of which" the true proof itself ought to be tested. For these reasons he also who asks us **54** to believe those who are in a natural state, but not those whose disposition is nonnatural, will be acting absurdly; for he will not gain credence if he says this without proof, and, for the reasons given above, he will not possess a true and approved proof.

And even were one to concede that the sense **55** impressions of those in a natural state were reliable, and those of men in a nonnatural condition unreliable, even so the judgment of external real objects by means of the senses alone will be found to be impossible. For certainly the sense of sight, even when it is in a natural state, pronounces the same tower to be at one time round, at another square; and the sense of taste declares the same food to be unpleasant in the case of those full-fed, but pleasant in the case of those who are hungry; and the sense of hearing likewise perceives the same sound as loud by night

56 but as faint by day; and the sense of smell regards the same objects as malodorous in the case of most people, but not so in the case of tanners; and the same sense of touch feels warmth in the outer hall, when we enter the bathrooms, but cold when we leave them. Therefore, since even when in a natural state the senses contradict themselves, and their dispute is incapable of decision, seeing that we possess no accepted criterion by means of which it can be judged, the same perplexities must necessarily follow. Moreover, for the establishment of this conclusion we may derive still further arguments from our previous discussion of the modes of suspension. Hence it would probably be untrue to say that sense perception alone is able to judge real external objects.

57   Let us, then, proceed in our exposition to the intellect. Now those who claim that we should attend to the intellect only in our judgment of things will, in the first place, be unable to show that the existence of the intellect is apprehensible. For when Gorgias,* in denying that anything exists, denies also the existence of the intellect, while some declare that it has real existence, how will they decide this contradiction? Not by the intellect, for so they will be assuming the matter in question; nor yet by anything else, since, as they assert, according to our present assumption there exists nothing else by means of which objects are judged. So then the problem as to whether intellect does or does not exist will not admit of decision

---

*[Ca. 483–376 B.C. Sophist and rhetor immortalized in Plato's *Gorgias*.]

or apprehension; and from this it follows, as a corollary, that in the judgment of objects we ought not to attend to the intellect alone, which has not as yet been apprehended.

But let it be granted that the intellect has been **58** apprehended, and let us agree, by way of assumption, that it really exists; I still affirm that it cannot judge objects. For if it does not even discern itself accurately but contradicts itself about its own existence and the mode of its origin and the position in which it is placed, how can it be able to apprehend anything else accurately? And even if it be granted that the **59** intellect is capable of judging objects, we shall not discover how to judge according to it. For since there exists great divergence in respect of the intellect— for the intellect of Gorgias, according to which he states that nothing exists, is one kind, and another kind is that of Heracleitus, according to which he declares that all things exist, and another that of those who say that some things do and others do not exist— we shall have no means of deciding between these divergent intellects, nor shall we be able to assert that it is right to take this man's intellect as our guide but not that man's. For if we venture to judge by **60** any one intellect, by thus agreeing to assent to one side in the dispute we shall be assuming the matter in question; while if we judge by anything else, we shall be falsifying the assertion that one ought to judge objects by the intellect alone.

Further, we shall be able to show, from the state- **61** ments made concerning the criterion "By whom" (as it is called), that we are unable to discover the intellect that is cleverer than all the others; and also that if we should discover the intellect that is cleverer than

62 past and present intellects we ought not to attend to it, since it is not evident whether yet another intellect may not arise which is cleverer than it; and further, that even if we assume an intellect which none could possibly surpass, we shall not assent to the man who judges by means of it, dreading lest he may put forward some false statement and succeed in persuading us of its truth because he possesses the keenest intellect. Neither, then, by the intellect alone ought we to judge objects.

63 The only remaining alternative is judgment by means of both senses and intellect. But this again is impossible; for not only do the senses not guide the intellect to apprehension, but they even oppose it. For it is certain, at any rate, that from the fact that honey appears bitter to some and sweet to others, Democritus declared that it is neither sweet nor bitter, while Heracleitus said that it is both. And the same account may be given of all the other senses and sensibles. Thus, when it starts out from the senses, the intellect is compelled to make diverse and conflicting statements; and this is alien to a criterion of apprehension.

64 Then there is this also to be said: they will judge objects either by all the senses and by all men's intellects or by some. But if a man shall say "by all," he will be claiming what is impossible in view of the immense discrepancy which obviously exists amongst the senses and the intellects; and moreover, by reason of the assertion of Gorgias's intellect that "we must not give heed either to sense or to intellect," the man's statement will be demolished. And if they shall say "by some," how will they decide that we ought to give heed to these senses and this intellect and not to those, seeing that they possess no accepted criterion by which to judge the differing senses and intellects? And if they shall say that we will judge **65** the senses and the intellects by the intellect and the senses, they are assuming the matter in question; for what we are questioning is the possibility of judging by means of these.

Another point we must make is this: either one **66** will judge both the senses and the intellects by the senses, or both the senses and the intellects by the intellects, or the senses by the senses and the intellect by the intellects, or the intellects by the senses and the senses by the intellect. If then they shall propose to judge both objects by the senses or by the intellect, they will no longer be judging by sense and intellect but by one of these two, whichever one they may choose, and thus they will be entangled in the perplexities previously mentioned. And if they shall judge **67** the senses by the senses and the intellects by the intellect, then, since both senses conflict with senses and intellects with intellects, whichever of the conflicting senses they shall adopt for judging the rest of the senses, they will be assuming the matter in question; for they will be adopting one section of the series in dispute, as being already reliable, to decide about the others which, equally with it, are in question. And

68 the same argument applies to the intellects. And if they shall judge the intellects by the senses, and the senses by the intellect, this involves circular reasoning inasmuch as it is required that the intellects should be judged first in order that the senses may be judged, and the senses be first scrutinized in order that the **69** intellects may be tested. Since, therefore, criteria of the one species cannot be judged by those of a like species, nor those of both the species by those of one species, nor conversely by those of an unlike species, we shall not be able to prefer intellect to intellect or sense to sense. And because of this we shall have nothing by which to judge; for if we shall be unable to judge by all the senses and intellects, and shall not know either by which of them we ought and by which we ought not to judge, then we shall possess no means by which to judge objects.

Consequently, for these reasons also the criterion "By means of which" will have no real existence.

CHAPTER VII. OF THE CRITERION "ACCORDING TO WHICH"

70 Let us consider next the criterion "According to which," as they* say, objects are judged. In the first place, then, we may say this of it, that "presentation" is inconceivable. They declare that "presentation" is an impression on "the regent part." Since, then, the soul, and the regent part, is breath or something more subtle than breath, as they affirm,

---

*The Stoics.

no one will be able to conceive of an impression upon it either by way of depression and eminence, as we see in the case of seals, or by way of the magical "alteration" they talk about; for the soul will not be able to conserve the remembrance of all the concepts that compose an art, since the preexisting concepts are obliterated by the subsequent "alterations." Yet **71** even if "presentation" could be conceived, it would still be nonapprehensible; for since it is an affection of the regent part, and the regent part, as we have shown, is not apprehended, neither shall we apprehend its affection.

Further, even were we to grant that the "presen- **72** tation" is apprehended, objects cannot be judged according to it; for the intellect, as they assert, does not make contact with external objects and receive presentations by means of itself but by means of the senses, and the senses do not apprehend external real objects but only, if at all, their own affections.* So then the presentation will be that of the affection of the sense, which is different from the external reality; for honey is not the same as my feeling of sweetness nor gall the same as my feeling of bitterness, but a different thing. And if this affection differs from **73** the external real object, the presentation will not be that of the external reality but of something else which is different therefrom. If, therefore, the intellect judges according to this, it judges badly and not according to reality. Consequently, it is absurd to say that ex-

---

*I.e., sensations or feelings.

ternal objects are to be judged according to the presentation.

74   Nor, again, is it possible to assert that the soul apprehends external realities by means of the affections of sense owing to the similarity of the affections of the senses to the external real objects. For how is the intellect to know whether the affections of the senses are similar to the objects of sense when it has not itself encountered the external objects, and the senses do not inform it about their real nature but only about their own affections, as I have argued **75** from the modes of suspension? For just as the man who does not know Socrates but has seen a picture of him does not know whether the picture is like Socrates, so also the intellect when it gazes on the affections of the senses but does not behold the external objects will not so much as know whether the affections of the senses are similar to the external realities. So that not even on the ground of resemblance will he be able to judge these objects according to the presentation.

76   But let us grant by way of concession that in addition to being conceived and apprehended the presentation is also such that it admits of objects being judged according to it, although the argument points to an entirely opposite conclusion. In this case we shall either believe every presentation, or impression, and judge according thereto, or some one impression. But if we are to believe every impression, clearly we shall believe also that of Xeniades according to which he asserted that all impressions are untrustworthy, and our statement will be reversed and made to say that all impressions are not of such a sort that objects can be judged according to them. And **77** if we are to believe some, how shall we decide that it is proper to believe these and disbelieve those? For if they say we are to do so without presentation, they will be granting that presentation is superfluous for judging, inasmuch as they will be stating that objects can be judged without it; while if they say "by the aid of presentation," how will they select the presentation which they are adopting for the purpose of judging all the other presentations? Once again **78** they will need a second presentation to judge the first, and a third to judge the second, and so on *ad infinitum.* But it is impossible to judge an infinite series; and therefore it is impossible to discover what sort of presentations we ought to employ as criteria, and what we ought not. Seeing, then, that, even should we grant that one ought to judge objects according to presentations, whether we adopt the alternative of trusting all as criteria or that of trusting some and distrusting others, in either case the argument is overthrown, and we are forced to conclude that we ought not to adopt presentations as criteria for the judging of objects.

This is enough to say now, in our outline sketch, **79** with reference to the criterion "According to which," as it was said, objects are judged. But one should notice that we do not propose to assert that the criterion of truth is unreal (for that would be dogmatism); but since the dogmatists appear to have established plausibly that there really is a criterion of truth, we have set up counterarguments which appear to be plausible; and though we do not positively affirm either that they are true or that they are more plausible than their opposites, yet because of the apparently equal plausibility of these arguments and of those propounded by the dogmatists we deduce suspension of judgment.

CHAPTER VIII. OF THE TRUE AND TRUTH

80 Even were we to grant, by way of hypothesis, that a criterion of truth exists, it is found to be useless and vain if we recall that, so far as the statements of the dogmatists go, truth is unreal and the true **81** nonsubstantial. The passage we recall is this: "The true is said to differ from truth in three ways—in essence, composition, potency. In essence, since the true is incorporeal (for it is judgment and 'expression'), while truth is a body (for it is knowledge declaratory of all true things, and knowledge is a particular state of the regent part, just as the fist is a particular state of the hand, and the regent part is a body; for according **82** to them it is breath). In composition, because the true is a simple thing, as for example 'I converse,' whereas truth is a compound of many true cognitions. In **83** potency, since truth depends on knowledge but the true does not altogether so depend. Consequently, as they say, truth exists only in the good man, but the true in the bad man as well; for it is possible for the bad man to utter something true."

Such are the statements of the dogmatists. But **84** we,—having regard here again to the plan of our treatise,—shall confine our present discussion to the true, since its refutation entails that of truth as well, it being defined as the "system of knowledge of things true." Again, since some of our arguments, whereby we dispute the very existence of the true, are more general, others of a specific kind, whereby we prove that the true does not exist in utterance or in expression or in the movement of the intellect, we deem it sufficient for the present to set forth only those of the more general kind. For just as, when the foundation of a wall collapses, all the superstructure collapses along with it, so also, when, the substantial existence of the true is refuted, all the particular inventions of the logic of the dogmatists are included in the refutation.

CHAPTER IX. DOES ANYTHING TRUE REALLY EXIST?

Seeing, then, that there is a controversy amongst the **85** dogmatists regarding "the true," since some assert that something true exists, others that nothing true exists, it is impossible to decide the controversy, because the man who says that something true exists will not be believed without proof, on account of the controversy; and if he wishes to offer proof, he will be disbelieved if he acknowledges that his proof is false, whereas if he declares that his proof is true he becomes involved in circular reasoning and will be required to show proof of the real truth of his proof, and another proof of that proof, and so on *ad infinitum*. But it is impossible to prove an infinite series; and so it is impossible also to get to know that something true exists.

86   Moreover, the "something," which is, they declare, the highest genus of all, is either true or false or neither false nor true or both false and true. If, then, they shall assert that it is false they will be confessing that all things are false. For just as it follows because "animal" is animate that all particular animals also are animate, so too if the highest genus of all ("something") is false all the particulars also will be false and nothing true. And this involves also the conclusion that nothing is false; for the very statements "all things are false," and "something false exists," being themselves included in the "all," will be false. And if the "something" is true, all things will be true; and from this again it follows that nothing is true, since this statement itself (I mean that "nothing is true") being "something" is true. And if

87 the "something" is both false and true, each of its particulars will be both false and true. From which we conclude that nothing is really true; for that which has its real nature such that it is true will certainly not be false. And if the "something" is neither false nor true, it is acknowledged that all the particulars also, being declared to be neither false nor true, will not be true. So for these reasons it will be nonevident to us whether the true exists.

88   Furthermore, the true things are either apparent only, or nonevident only, or in part nonevident and in part apparent*; but none of these alternatives is true, as we shall show; therefore nothing is true. If, however, the true things are apparent only, they will assert either that all or that some of the apparent are true. And if they say "all," the argument is overthrown; for it is apparent to some that nothing is true. If, again, they say "some," no one can assert without testing that these phenomena are true, those false, while if he employs a test or criterion he will say either that this criterion is apparent or that it is nonevident. But it is certainly not nonevident; for it is now being assumed† that the apparent objects only are true. And if it is apparent, since the matter in question is what apparent things are true and what false, that apparent thing which is adopted for the purpose of judging the apparent objects will itself in turn require an apparent criterion, and this again another, and so on *ad infinitum*. But it is impossible to judge an infinite series; and hence it is impossible to apprehend whether the true things are apparent only.

89

Similarly also he who declares that the nonevident only are true will not imply that they are all true (for he will not say that it is true that the stars are even in number and that they are also odd); while if some are true, whereby shall we decide that these nonevident things are true and those false? Certainly not by an apparent criterion; and if by a nonevident one, then since our problem is which of

90

---

*By "true things" are meant judgments or propositions that conform to fact.

†This is incorrect. On the hypothesis, nonevidents may also be true.

the nonevident things are true and which false, this nonevident criterion will itself also need another to judge it, and this again a third, and so on *ad infinitum.* Neither, then, are the true things nonevident only.

91   The remaining alternative is to say that of the true some are apparent, some nonevident; but this too is absurd. For either all the apparent and all the nonevident are true, or some of the apparent and some of the nonevident. If, then, we say "all," the argument will again be overthrown, since the truth is granted of the statement "nothing is true," and the truth will be asserted of both the statements "the stars are even in number" and "they are odd." But **92** if some of the apparent are true and some of the nonevident, how shall we judge that of the apparent these are true but those false? For if we do so by means of an apparent thing, the argument is thrown back *ad infinitum;* and if by means of a thing nonevident, then, since the nonevidents also require to be judged, by what means is this nonevident thing to be judged? If by an apparent thing, we fall into circular reasoning; and if by a thing nonevident, into **93** the regress *ad infinitum.* And about the nonevident we must make a similar statement; for he who attempts to judge them by something nonevident is thrown back *ad infinitum,* while he who judges by a thing apparent or with the constant assistance of a thing apparent falls back *ad infinitum,* or, if he passes over to the apparent, is guilty of circular reasoning. It is false, therefore, to say that of the true some are apparent, some nonevident.

If, then, neither the apparent nor the nonevident **94** alone are true, nor yet some apparent and some nonevident things, nothing is true. But if nothing is true, and the criterion seems to require the true for the purpose of judging, the criterion is useless and vain, even if we grant, by way of concession, that it possesses some substantial reality. And if we have to suspend judgment as to whether anything true exists, it follows that those who declare that "dialectic is the science of things true and false and neither" speak rashly.

And since the criterion of truth has appeared **95** to be unattainable, it is no longer possible to make positive assertions either about those things which (if we may depend on the statements of the dogmatists) seem to be evident or about those which are nonevident; for since the dogmatists suppose they apprehend the latter from the things evident, if we are forced to suspend judgment about the evident, how shall we dare to make pronouncements about the nonevident? Yet, by way of superaddition, we **96** shall also raise separate objections against the nonevident class of objects. And since they seem to be apprehended and confirmed by means of sign and proof, we shall show briefly that it is proper to suspend judgment also about sign and proof. We will begin with sign; for indeed proof seems to be a kind of sign.

Chapter X. Concerning Sign

97 Of objects, then, some, according to the dogmatists,* are preevident, some nonevident; and of the nonevident, some are altogether nonevident, some occasionally nonevident, some naturally nonevident. Preevident are, as they assert, those which come to our knowledge of themselves, as for example the fact that it is daytime; altogether nonevident are those which are not of a nature to fall within our apprehension, as that the stars are even in number; occa-

98 sionally nonevident are those which, though patent in their nature, are occasionally rendered nonevident to us owing to certain external circumstances,† as the city of Athens is now to me; naturally nonevident are those which are not of such a nature as to fall within our clear perception, like the intelligible pores; for these never appear of themselves but may be thought to be apprehended, if at all, owing to other things, such as perspirations or something of the sort.

99 Now the preevident objects, they say, do not require a sign, for they are apprehended of themselves. And neither do the altogether nonevident, since of course they are not even apprehended at all. But such objects as are occasionally or naturally nonevident are apprehended by means of signs—not of course by the same signs, but by "suggestive" signs in the case of

---

*I.e., the Stoics.

†I.e., distance in space. From this we infer that Sextus was not then residing at Athens.

the occasionally nonevident and by "indicative" signs in the case of the naturally nonevident.

Of the signs, then, according to them, some are **100** suggestive, some indicative. They term a sign "suggestive" when, being mentally associated with the thing signified, it by its clearness at the time of its perception, though the thing signified remains nonevident, suggests to us the thing associated with it, which is not clearly perceived at the moment—as for instance in the case of smoke and fire. An "in- **101** dicative" sign, they say, is that which is not clearly associated with the thing signified, but signifies that whereof it is a sign by its own particular nature and constitution, just as, for instance, the bodily motions are signs of the soul. Hence, too, they define this sign as follows: "An indicative sign is an antecedent judgment, in a sound hypothetical syllogism, which serves to reveal the consequent." Seeing, then, that **102** there are, as we have said, two different kinds of sign, we do not argue against every sign but only against the indicative kind as it seems to be invented by the dogmatists. For the suggestive sign is relied on by living experience, since when a man sees smoke fire is signified, and when he beholds a scar he says that there has been a wound. Hence, not only do we not fight against living experience, but we even lend it our support by assenting undogmatically to what it relies on, while opposing the private inventions of the dogmatists.

These prefatory remarks it was, perhaps, fitting **103** to make for the sake of elucidating the object of our inquiry. It remains for us to proceed to our refutation, not in any anxiety to show that the indicative sign is wholly unreal, but reminding ourselves of the apparent equivalence of the arguments adduced for its reality and for its unreality.

CHAPTER XI. DOES AN INDICATIVE SIGN EXIST?

104 Now the sign, judging by the statements of the dogmatists about it, is inconceivable. Thus, for instance, the Stoics, who seem to have defined it exactly, in attempting to establish the conception of the sign, state that "A sign is an antecedent judgment in a valid hypothetical syllogism, which serves to reveal the consequent"; and "judgment" they define as "A self-complete expression which is of itself declaratory"; and "valid hypothetical syllogism" as one "which does not begin with truth and end with a false consequent."

105 For either the syllogism begins with the true and ends with the true (*e.g.,* "If there is day, there is light"), or it begins with what is false and ends in falsehood (like "If the earth flies, the earth is winged"), or it begins with truth and ends in falsehood (like "If the earth exists, the earth flies"), or it begins with falsehood and ends in truth (like "If the earth flies, the earth exists"). And they say that of these only that which begins with truth and ends in falsehood is

106 invalid, and the rest valid. "Antecedent," they say, is "the precedent clause in a hypothetical syllogism which begins in truth and ends in truth." And it "serves to reveal the consequent," since in the syllogism "If this woman has milk, she has conceived," the clause "If this woman has milk" seems to be evidential of the clause "she has conceived."

Such is the Stoic doctrine. But we assert, firstly, **107** that it is nonevident whether any "expression" exists. For since some of the dogmatists, the Epicureans, declare that expression does not exist, others, the Stoics, that it does exist, when the Stoics assert its existence they are employing either mere assertion or demonstration as well. If assertion, then the Epicureans will confute them with the assertion which states that no expression exists. But if they shall adduce demonstration, then since demonstration is composed of expressed judgments, and because it is composed of expressions will be unable to be adduced to confirm the existence of expression (for how will he who refuses to allow the existence of expression grant the reality of a system compounded of expressions?),—it follows that the man who attempts to **108** establish the existence of expression from the reality of the system of expressions is proposing to confirm the problematic by the problematic. If, then, it is impossible to establish either simply or by means of demonstration that any expression exists, it is nonevident that any expression exists.

So, too, with the question whether judgment exists; for the judgment is a form of expression. And very possibly, even should it be granted by way of **109** assumption that expression exists, judgment will be found to be nonexistent, it being compounded of expressions not mutually coexistent. Thus, for example, in the case of "If day exists, light exists," when I say "day exists" the clause "light exists" is not yet in existence, and when I say "light exists" the clause "day exists" is no longer in existence. If then it is impossible for things compounded of certain parts to be really existent if those parts do not mutually coexist, and if the parts whereof the judgment is composed do not mutually coexist, then the judgment will have no real existence.

But passing over this objection, it will be found that the valid hypothetical syllogism is nonapprehensible. For Philo* says that a valid hypothetical syllogism is "that which does not begin with a truth and end with a falsehood," as for instance the syllogism "If it is day, I converse," when in fact it is day and I am conversing; but Diodorus defines it as "that which neither was nor is capable of beginning with a truth and ending with a falsehood"; so that according to him the syllogism now mentioned seems to be false, since if it is in fact day but I have remained silent it will begin with a truth but end

111 with a falsehood, whereas the syllogism "If atomic elements of things do not exist, atomic elements exist," seems true, since it begins with the false clause "atomic elements do not exist" and will end, according to him, with the true clause "atomic elements exist." And those who introduce "connection," or "coherence," assert that it is a valid hypothetical syllogism whenever the opposite of its consequent contradicts

---

*A Megaric philosopher (fl. ca. 300 B.C.), not the Academic mentioned in Book I, chapter 33.

its antecedent clause; so that, according to them, the above-mentioned syllogisms are invalid, whereas the syllogism "If day exists, day exists" is true. And those who judge by "implication" declare that a hypothetical **112** syllogism is true when its consequent is potentially included in its antecedent; and according to them the syllogism "If day exists, day exists," and every such duplicated syllogism, will probably be false; for it is not feasible that any object should itself be included in itself.

Probably, then, it will not seem feasible to get **113** this controversy resolved. For whether we prefer any one of the above-mentioned rival views without proof or by the aid of proof, in neither case shall we gain credence. For proof itself is held to be valid whenever its conclusion follows the combination of its premises as the consequent follows the antecedent; thus, for example—"If it is day it is light; but in fact it is day; therefore it is light": ["If it is day it is light," "it is day and also it is light."]* But when we inquire **114** how we are to judge the logical sequence of the consequent in its relation to the antecedent, we are met with the argument in a circle. For in order to prove the judgment upon the hypothetical syllogism, the conclusion of the proof must follow logically from its premises, as we said above; and, in turn, in order to establish this, the hypothetical syllogism and its logical sequence must be tested; and this is absurd.

---

*The words bracketed give an unintelligible form of syllogism, and the Greek text is evidently corrupt. Possibly we should read: "It is day; and if it is day it is light; therefore, it is light."

115 So then the valid hypothetical syllogism is nonapprehensible.

But the "antecedent" also is unintelligible. For the antecedent, as they assert, is "the leading clause in a hypothetical syllogism of the kind which begins **116** with a truth and ends in a truth." But if the sign serves to reveal the consequent, the consequent is either preevident or nonevident. If, then, it is preevident, it will not so much as need the thing which is to reveal it but will be apprehended along with it and will not be the object signified thereby, and hence also the thing mentioned will not be a "sign" of the object. But if the consequent is nonevident, seeing that there exists an unsettled controversy about things nonevident, as to which of them are true, which false, and in general whether any of them is true, it will be nonevident whether the hypothetical syllogism ends in a true consequent. And this involves the further fact that it is nonevident whether the leading clause in the syllogism is the logical ante-**117** cedent. But to pass over this objection also, the sign cannot serve to reveal the consequent, if the thing signified is relative to the sign and is, therefore, apprehended along with it. For relatives are apprehended along with each other; and just as "right" cannot be apprehended as "right of left" before "left," nor *vice versa*—and the same holds good of all other relative terms,—so neither will it be possible for the sign, as "sign of signified," to be apprehended before **118** the thing signified. And if the sign is not apprehended before the thing signified, neither can it really serve to reveal the actual thing which is apprehended along with itself and not after itself.

Thus also, so far as we may judge by the usual statements of the dissenting philosophers (the Stoics), the sign is inconceivable. For they assert that it is both relative and serving to reveal the thing signified, **119** in relation to which they say it was. Accordingly, if it is relative and in relation to the thing signified it certainly ought to be apprehended along with the thing signified, as is "left" with "right," "up" with "down," and the rest of the relative terms. Whereas, if it serves to reveal the thing signified, it certainly ought to be apprehended before it, in order that by being foreknown it may lead us to a conception of the object which comes to be known by means of it. But it is impossible to form a conception of an **120** object which cannot be known before the thing before which it must necessarily be apprehended; and so it is impossible to conceive of an object which is both relative and also really serves to reveal the thing in relation to which it is thought. But the sign is, as they affirm, both relative and serving to reveal the thing signified; wherefore it is impossible to conceive of the sign.

Furthermore, there is this also to be said. **121** Amongst our predecessors there existed a controversy, some declaring that an indicative sign exists, others maintaining that no indicative sign exists. He, then, who asserts the existence of an indicative sign will assert it either simply and without proof, making a bald assertion, or by the aid of proof. But if he shall employ mere assertion he will not gain credence; while if he shall propose to prove it he will be assuming **122** the matter in question. For since proof is stated to come under the genus sign, seeing that it is disputed whether or not a sign exists, there will also be a dispute as to whether proof does or does not at all exist—just as, when we make, let us suppose, the inquiry "Does animal exist?" we are inquiring also "Does man exist?" But it is absurd to try to prove the matter in question either by means of what is equally in question or by means of itself. So that neither will one be able by means of proof to affirm **123** positively that sign exists. And if it is not possible either simply or with the aid of proof to make a positive declaration about the sign, it is impossible to make an apprehensive affirmation concerning it; and if the sign is not apprehended with exactness, neither will it be said to be significant of anything, inasmuch as there is no agreement even about itself; and because of this it will not even be a sign. Hence, according to this line of reasoning also, the sign will be unreal and inconceivable.

124 But there is this further to be said. Either the signs are apparent only or nonevident only, or some are apparent and some nonevident. But none of these alternatives is valid; therefore sign does not exist.

Now that all the signs are not nonevident is shown by the following argument. The nonevident does not become apparent of itself, as the dogmatists assert, but is perceived by means of something else. The sign, therefore, if it were nonevident, would require another nonevident sign—since, according to the hypothesis assumed, there is no apparent sign—and this again a third, and so on *ad infinitum*. But it is impossible to grasp an infinite series of signs; and so it is impossible for the sign to be apprehended when it is nonevident. And for this reason it will also be unreal, as it is unable to signify anything and to be a sign owing to its not being apprehended.

And if all the signs are apparent, then, because **125** the sign is a relative thing and in relation to the thing signified, and relatives are apprehended conjointly, the things said to be signified, being apprehended along with what is apparent, will be apparent. For just as when the right and left are perceived together, the right is not said to appear more than the left nor the left than the right, so when the sign and the thing signified are apprehended together the sign should not be said to appear any more than the thing signified. And if the thing signified is apparent, it **126** will not even be signified, as it requires nothing to signify and reveal it. Hence, just as when "right" is abolished there exists no "left," so when the thing signified is abolished there can exist no sign, so that the sign is found to be unreal, if one should declare that the signs are apparent only.

It remains to declare that of the signs some are **127** apparent, others nonevident; but even so the difficulties remain. For the things said to be signified by the apparent signs will, as we said before, be apparent and require nothing to signify them, and will not even be things signified at all, so that neither will the signs be signs, as not signifying anything.

128 And as to the nonevident signs which need things to reveal them, if we say that they are signified by things nonevident, the argument will be involved in a regress *ad infinitum,* rendering them nonapprehensible and therefore unreal, as we said before; whereas, if they are to be signified by things apparent, they will be apparent, because apprehended along with their apparent signs, and therefore also unreal. For it is impossible for any object really to exist which is by nature both nonevident and apparent; but the signs which we are discussing, though assumed to be nonevident, have been found to be apparent owing to the reversal of the argument.

129 If, therefore, the signs are neither all apparent nor all nonevident, nor yet some of the signs apparent and some nonevident, and besides these there is no other alternative, as they themselves affirm, then the so-called signs will be unreal.

130 So then these few arguments out of many will be enough for the present to suggest to us the non-existence of an indicative sign. Next, we shall set forth those which go to suggest the existence of a sign, in order that we may exhibit the equipollence of the counterbalancing arguments.

Either, then, the phrases used in criticism of the

sign signify something or they signify nothing.* But
if they are nonsignificant how could they affect the
reality of the sign? While if they signify something,
there exists a sign. Further, the arguments against **131**
the sign are either probative or nonprobative; but
if they are nonprobative they do not prove the nonexistence of a sign; while if they are probative, since
proof, as serving to reveal the conclusion, belongs
to the genus sign, sign will exist. Whence this argument also is propounded: "If sign exists, sign exists;
and if sign exists not, sign exists; for the nonexistence
of sign is shown by proof, which is a form of sign.
But sign either exists or exists not; therefore sign
exists." And this argument is counterbalanced by the **132**
following argument: "If any sign does not exist, sign
does not exist; and if sign is that which the dogmatists
declare sign to be, sign does not exist (for the sign
under discussion, according to the conception of it
and as stated to be both relative and serving to reveal
the thing signified, is found to be unreal, as we have
shown). But sign either exists or exists not; therefore **133**
sign does not exist."

Regarding also the phrases used in support of

---

*Cf. *Against the Logicians,* ii. 279. The meaning of these sections, 130–
133, is briefly this: The dogmatists argue (1) that the skeptics' objections
to "sign" must signify either something or nothing; if nothing, they have
no force against it, while if they signify something they are signs themselves
and so prove sign's existence; (2) the arguments against "sign" prove either
something or nothing; if nothing, they fail to prove the nonexistence of
"sign," while if they prove something, they are proofs, i.e., a species of
"sign," and thus prove sign's existence. Hence, whichever view we take—
the dogmatists' that "sign exists," or the skeptics' that "sign exists not"—
we arrive at the same conclusion that "sign exists."

the sign,* let the dogmatists themselves say in reply to our argument whether they signify something or signify nothing. For if they signify nothing, the existence of sign is not confirmed; whereas if they signify something, the thing signified will follow them; and it was "the existence of a sign." And from this follows, as we have shown, the nonexistence of sign, because of the reversal of the argument.

In short, then, since such plausible arguments are adduced both for the existence and for the nonexistence of sign, we must declare that sign is "no more" existent than nonexistent.

CHAPTER XII. OF PROOF

134 Now it is plain from this that neither is proof a matter upon which there is agreement; for if we suspend judgment about the sign, and proof also is a sign, we must necessarily suspend judgment about proof likewise. And in fact we shall find that the arguments propounded concerning the sign can be adapted to apply to proof as well, since it seems to be both relative and serving to reveal the conclusion, and from these properties followed nearly all the results we mentioned in the case of the sign.

135 If, however, one ought to devote a separate discussion to proof, I shall proceed to treat of it concisely after

---

*In this § 133 the skeptics are replying to the first argument of the dogmatists (in § 130); the conclusion that the existence of "sign" proves its nonexistence is based on the arguments in § 132, which "reverses" that of the dogmatists.

endeavoring first to explain shortly the definition they give of proof.

Proof is, they assert, "an argument which, by means of agreed premises, reveals by way of deduction a nonevident inference." What their statement means will be made clearer by what follows. "An argument is a system composed of premises and an inference. The premises of it are (it is said) the judgments **136** adopted by consent for the establishment of the inference, and the inference is the judgment established by the premises." For example, in the argument "If it is day, it is light; but it is in truth day; therefore it is light," the clause "therefore it is light" is a conclusion, and the rest are premises. And of arguments **137** some are conclusive, some inconclusive—conclusive when the hypothetical syllogism which begins with the combination made by the premises of the argument and ends with its inference is valid; thus, for example, the argument just stated is conclusive since the combination of its premises—"it is day" and "if it is day, it is light"—is followed by "it is light" in the syllogism "It is day, and if it is day it is light; therefore it it light." But arguments that are not like this are inconclusive.

And of the conclusive arguments some are true, **138** some not true—true when not only the syllogism formed by the combination of the premises and the inference is valid,* as we said above, but the conclusion also and the combination of the premises,

---

*"Valid" refers only to logical form; "true" to content.

which is the antecedent in the syllogism, is really true. And a combination is true when it has all its parts true, as in the case of "It is day, and if it is day, it is light"; but those of a different kind are not true.

139 For an argument such as this—"If it is night, it is dark; but in fact it is night; therefore it is dark"— is indeed conclusive, since the syllogism "It is night, and if it is night it is dark, therefore it is dark" is a valid one, but, when it is daytime, it is not true. For the antecedent combination—"it is night, and if it is night it is dark"—is false since it contains the falsehood "it is night"; for the combination which contains a falsehood is false. Hence they also say that a true argument is that which deduces a true conclusion from true premises.

140   Of true arguments, again, some are "probative," some "nonprobative"; and the probative are those which deduce something nonevident by means of preevident premises, the nonprobative those not of this sort. For example, an argument such as this— "If it is day it is light; but in fact it is day; therefore it is light" is not probative; for its conclusion, that "it is light," is preevident. But an argument like this— "If sweat pours through the surface, there are insensible pores; but in fact sweat does pour through the surface; therefore there are insensible pores"— is a probative one, as its conclusion ("there are therefore insensible pores") is nonevident.

141   And of arguments which deduce something non-evident, some conduct us through the premises to the conclusion by way of progression only, others both by way of progression and by way of discovery as well. By progression, for instance, are those which seem to depend on belief and memory, such as the argument "If a god has said to you that this man will be rich, this man will be rich; but this god (assume that I point to Zeus) has said to you that this man will be rich; therefore he will be rich"; for we assent to the conclusion not so much on account of the logical force of the premises as because of our belief in the statement of the god. But some arguments **142** conduct us to the conclusion by way of discovery as well as of progression, like the following: "If sweat pours through the surface, there are insensible pores; but the first is true, therefore also the second"; for the pouring of the sweat makes discovery of the fact of the existence of pores, because of the prior assumption that moisture cannot pass through a solid body.

So, then, proof ought to be an argument which **143** is deductive and true and has a nonevident conclusion which is discovered by the potency of the premises; and because of this, proof is defined as "an argument which by means of agreed premises discovers by way of deduction a nonevident inference." It is in these terms, then, that they are in the habit of explaining the conception of proof.

CHAPTER XIII. DOES PROOF EXIST?

That proof has no existence may be inferred from **144** their own statements, by refuting each of the assumptions implied in its conception. Thus, for instance, the argument is compounded of judgments, but compound things cannot exist unless its component elements mutually coexist, as is preevident from the case of a bed and similar objects; but the parts of an argument do not mutually coexist. For when we are stating the first premise, neither the second premise nor the inference is as yet in existence; and when we are stating the second premise, the first is no longer existent and the inference is not yet existent; and when we announce the inference, its premises are no longer in being. Therefore the parts of the argument do not mutually coexist; and hence the argument too will seem to be nonexistent.

145 But apart from this, the conclusive argument is nonapprehensible; for if it is judged by the coherence of the hypothetical premise, and the coherence in that premise is a matter of unsettled dispute and is probably nonapprehensible, as we suggested in our chapter (xi) "On the Sign," then the conclusive argument also will be nonapprehensible. Now the dialecticians* assert that an argument is inconclusive owing to inconsistency or to deficiency or to its being propounded in a bad form or to redundancy. An example of inconsistency is when the premises are not logically coherent with each other and with the inference, as in the argument "If it is day, it is light; but in fact wheat is being sold in the market; therefore Dion is walking." And it is a case of redundancy when we find a premise that is superfluous for the

146

147

---

*I.e., the Stoics.

logic of the argument, as for instance, "If it is day, it is light; but in fact it is day and Dion also is walking; therefore it is light." And it is due to the bad form in which it is propounded when the form of the argument is not conclusive; for whereas the really syllogistic arguments are, they say, such as these: "If it is day, it is light; but in fact it is day; therefore it is light"; and "If it is day, it is light; but it is not light; therefore it is not day,"—the inconclusive argument runs thus: "If it is day, it is light; but in fact it is light; therefore it is day." For since the major **148** premise announces that if its antecedent exists its consequent also exists, naturally when the antecedent is admitted the consequent also is inferred, and when the consequent is denied the antecedent also is denied; for if the antecedent had existed, the consequent also would have existed. But when the consequent is admitted, the antecedent is not necessarily admitted as well; for the major premise did not promise that the antecedent should follow the consequent, but only the consequent the antecedent.

Hence, the argument which deduces the con- **149** sequent from the major premise and the antecedent is said to be syllogistic,* and also that which deduces the opposite of the antecedent from the major premise and the opposite of the consequent; but the argument which, like that stated above, deduces the antecedent from the major premise and the consequent is inconclusive, so that it makes a false deduction, even

---

*(In Stoic terminology) definitely valid and conclusive.

though its premises are true, whenever it is uttered by lamplight at night. For though the major premise "If it is day, it is light" is true, and also the minor premise, "but in fact it is light," the inference "therefore 150 it is day" is false. And the argument is faulty by deficiency, when it suffers from the omission of some factor needed for the deducing of the conclusion: thus, for instance, while we have, as they think, a valid argument in "Wealth is either good or bad or indifferent; but it is neither bad nor indifferent; therefore it is good," the following is faulty by way of deficiency: "Wealth is either good or bad; but it 151 is not bad; therefore it is good." If, then, I shall show that, according to them, it is impossible to distinguish any difference between the inconclusive and the conclusive arguments, I shall have shown that the conclusive argument is nonapprehensible, so that their endless disquisitions on "dialectic" are superfluous. And I show it in this wise.

152   It was said that the argument which is inconclusive owing to inconsistency is recognized by the want of coherence which marks its premises in their relation both to each other and to the inference. Since, then, the recognition of this coherence ought to be preceded by the judgment on the hypothetical syllogism,* and that syllogism, as I have argued, does not admit of judgment, the argument that is inconclusive through inconsistency will likewise be in- 153 capable of being distinguished. For he who declares

---

*I.e., the syllogism as a whole, which is a "combination" of premises and conclusion.

that any particular argument is inconclusive through inconsistency will, if he is merely uttering a statement, find himself opposed by a statement which contradicts his own; while if he tries to prove it by argument, he will be told that this argument of his must itself be conclusive before he can prove that the premises or the argument said to be inconsistent are devoid of consistency. But we shall not know whether it is probative, since we have no agreed test of the syllogism whereby to judge whether the conclusion follows the logical connection formed by the premises. And thus, also, we shall be unable to distinguish the argument that is faulty through inconsistency from those that are conclusive.

And we will make the same reply to the man **154** who says that an argument is unsound owing to its being propounded in a faulty form; for he who maintains that a form is unsound will have no argument agreed to be conclusive whereby he will be able to draw the conclusion he states. And hereby we have **155** also potentially refuted those who try to show that there are arguments which are inconclusive through deficiency. For if the complete and finished argument is indistinguishable from others, the deficient also will be nonevident. And, further, he who proposes to prove by argument that a certain argument is deficient, seeing that he has no agreed test of a hypothetical syllogism whereby he can judge the coherence of the argument he is talking about, will be unable to make a tested and true pronouncement that it is deficient.

Moreover, the argument that is said to be faulty **156**

through redundancy is indistinguishable from those that are probative. For, so far as concerns redundancy, even the "nondemonstrable" arguments* so much talked of by the Stoics will be found to be inconclusive, and if they are demolished the whole of dialectic is overturned; for they are the arguments which, they say, need no proof to establish them, and themselves serve as proofs of the conclusiveness of the other arguments. And that they are redundant will be clear when we have set forth these nonprobative arguments and thus confirm our statement by reasoning.

157   Now there are, in their imaginings, many nondemonstrable arguments, but the five which they chiefly propound, and to which all the rest can, it seems, be referred, are these. The first is that which deduces the consequent from the major premise and the antecedent, as for example, "If it is day, it is light; but in fact it is day; therefore it is light." The second is that which deduces the opposite of the antecedent from the major premise and the opposite of the consequent, as for example, "If it is day, it is light; but it is not light; therefore it is not day."

158 The third deduces from the negation of a coupled premise and the affirmation of one of its clauses the opposite of the other clause, as for example, "It is not both night and day; but it is day; therefore it is not night." The fourth deduces from a disjunctive premise and one of its alternative clauses the opposite of the other, as for example, "Either it is day or

---

*Those which need no proof as being self-evident.

it is night; but it is day; therefore it is not night."
The fifth deduces from a disjunctive premise and the
opposite of one of its clauses the other clause, as
for example, "Either it is day or it is night; but it
is not night; therefore it is day."

These, then, are the much talked-of nondemon- **159**
strable arguments, but they all seem to me to be
inconclusive through redundancy. Thus for instance,
to begin with the first, either it is agreed, or else
it is nonevident, that in the major premise "If it is
day, it is light," the clause "it is light" follows from
its antecedent "it is day." But if this is nonevident,
we shall not grant the major premise as agreed; if,
however, it is preevident that if the clause "it is day"
be true, the clause "it is light" will necessarily be true
also, then, once we have asserted that "it is day,"
the statement "it is light" is also inferred, so that
an argument in the form "It is day, therefore it is
light" is sufficient, and the major premise "If it is
day, it is light" is redundant.

And in the case of the second nondemonstrable **160**
argument we make a similar objection. For it is either
possible or impossible for the antecedent to be true
when the consequent is not true. But if this is possible,
the major premise will not be valid; while if it is
impossible, at the moment of positing "Not the consequent" we posit also "Not the antecedent," and the
major premise is redundant once again, the argument propounded being "It is not light, therefore it
is not day."

The same reasoning applies also to the third non- **161**

demonstrable argument. For either it is preevident that it is impossible for the clauses in the coupled premise mutually to coexist, or else it is nonevident. And if it is nonevident we shall not grant the negative of the coupled premise; but if it is preevident, at the moment of positing the one clause the other is annulled, and the negative of the coupled premise is redundant when we propound the argument in the form "It is day, therefore it is not night."

162   And we deal in like manner with the fourth non-demonstrable argument and the fifth. For either it is preevident or it is nonevident that in the disjunctive premise one clause is true, the other false, in complete contradiction, as the disjunctive proclaims. And if this is nonevident, we shall not grant the disjunctive; but if it is preevident, if one of its clauses be affirmed it is apparent that the other is not true, and if one is negated it is preevident that the other is true, so that it is sufficient to frame the argument thus—"It is day, therefore it is not night," or "It is not day, therefore it is night"; and the disjunctive premise is redundant.

163   One may also make similar observations on the so-called "categorical" syllogisms, which are chiefly used by the Peripatetics. Thus, for example, in the argument—"The just is fair, but the fair is good, therefore the just is good," either it is agreed and preevident that "the fair is good," or it is disputed and is nonevident. But if it is nonevident, it will not be granted in the process of deduction, and consequently the syllogism will not be conclusive; while if it is preevident that whatsoever is fair is also without exception good, at the moment of stating that this particular thing is fair the fact that it is good is likewise implied, so that it is enough to put the argument in the form "The just is fair, therefore the just is good," and the other premise, in which it was stated that "the fair is good," is redundant. So too in an ar- **164** gument such as this—"Socrates is a man; every man is an animal; therefore Socrates is an animal,"—if it is not at once preevident that whatsoever is man is always also animal, the universal premise is not agreed, and neither will we admit it in the process of deduction. But if the fact that he is a man is logically followed **165** by the fact that he is also an animal, and in consequence the premise "Every man is an animal" is by agreement true, at the moment of stating that "Socrates is a man" we admit therewith that he is also an animal, so that an argument in the form "Socrates is a man, therefore Socrates is an animal" is sufficient, and the premise "Every man is an animal" is redundant. And **166** (not to dwell on the matter now) in the case of the other primary categorical arguments also it is possible to employ similar methods of reasoning.

Since, however, these arguments which the dialecticians lay down as the foundations of their syllogisms are redundant, by reason of this redundancy the whole of dialectic is thus far overthrown, seeing that we cannot distinguish the redundant, and consequently inconclusive, arguments from what are called the conclusive syllogisms. But if some persons **167** disapprove of arguments being of a "one-premise form," they deserve no more credence than does Antipater* who does not reject such arguments.

For these reasons, then, the argument named by the dialecticians "conclusive" is not judged acceptable. But further, the "true" argument is indiscoverable both for the foregoing reasons and because it ought in all cases to end in truth. For the conclusion which is said to be true is either apparent or nonevident. And **168** it is certainly not apparent; for it would not need to be disclosed by means of the premises if it were preceptible of itself and no less apparent than its premises. But if it is nonevident, then, since there is an unsettled dispute concerning things nonevident, as we mentioned above, and they are in consequence nonapprehensible, the conclusion also of the argument said to be true will be nonapprehensible. And if this is nonapprehensible, we shall not know whether the deduction is true or false. Thus we shall be in ignorance as to whether the argument is true or false, and the "true" argument will be indiscoverable.

169 But, to pass over these objections also, the argument which deduces what is nonevident by means of preevident premises is indiscoverable. For if the inference follows from the combination of its premises, and what follows and forms the consequent is relative and relative to the antecedent, and relatives are apprehended, as we have shown, simultaneously,—then, if the conclusion is nonevident, the premises also will be nonevident, while if the premises are

---

*[Antipater of Tarsus was head of the Stoic school ca. 150–130 B.C.]

preevident the conclusion also will be preevident, as being apprehended along with the preevident premises, so that no longer is there a deduction of what is nonevident from preevident premises. And for these **170** reasons, neither is the inference revealed by the premises, as it is either nonevident and not apprehended, or preevident and not in need of anything to reveal it. So that if proof is defined as "an argument which by deduction, that is conclusively, reveals a nonevident inference by means of certain premises agreed to be true," while we have shown that there exists no argument either conclusive or true or which deduces a nonevident conclusion by means of evident premises or serves to reveal its conclusion,—then it is apparent that proof is without real existence.

That proof is unreal, or even inconceivable, we **171** shall discover also from the following line of attack. He who asserts the existence of proof posits either a general or a particular proof; but, as we shall suggest, it is not possible to posit either the general or the particular proof; and besides these no other can be conceived; no one, therefore, can posit proof as really existing. Now the general proof is unreal for the fol- **172** lowing reasons. It either has or has not certain premises and a certain inference. And if it has them not, it is not even proof; while if it has premises and an inference, then, since everything which proves or is proved in this way belongs to the class of "particulars," proof will be particular; therefore no general proof exists. Nor yet any particular proof. For they will **173** describe as proof either the system made up of the premises and the inference or only the system of the premises; but neither of these is proof, as I shall show; **174** therefore particular proof does not exist. Now the system composed of the premises and the inference is not proof because, firstly, it contains a nonevident part—that is to say, the inference—and so will be nonevident, which is absurd; for if the proof is nonevident, instead of serving to prove other things it will itself be in need of something to prove it.

175 Moreover, since they assert that proof is a relative thing and relative to the inference, and relatives, as they themselves affirm, are conceived in relation to other things, the thing proved must be other than the proof; if, then, the thing proved is the conclusion, the proof will not be conceived along with the conclusion. For the conclusion either contributes something to its own proof or does not do so; but if it contributes, it will serve to reveal itself, while if it does not contribute but is redundant it will not be even a part of the proof, since we shall declare the proof to be faulty by reason of redundance. Nor **176** yet will the system composed of the premises by itself be proof; for who would maintain that a statement in the form "If it is day, it is light; but in fact it is day," either is an argument or completely expresses a piece of reasoning? So then, neither does the system of the premises alone constitute proof. Therefore the particular proof has no real existence either. But if neither the particular nor the general proof has real existence, and besides these one can conceive no other proof, then proof is without real existence.

And it is possible to show the unreality of proof **177** from these further considerations. If proof exists, either as apparent it serves to reveal what is apparent, or as nonevident what is nonevident, or as nonevident what is apparent, or as apparent what is nonevident; but it cannot be conceived as serving to reveal any of these; therefore it is inconceivable. For if it as **178** apparent serves to reveal the apparent, the thing revealed will be at once both apparent and nonevident—apparent because it was assumed to be such, and nonevident because it needs a revealer and is not clearly perceived by us of itself. And if as nonevident it reveals the nonevident, it will itself need something to reveal it and will not serve to reveal other things, which is foreign to the conception of proof. And for these reasons neither can there be **179** a nonevident proof of the preevident; nor yet a preevident proof of the nonevident; for since they are relatives, and relatives are apprehended together, that which is said to be proved, being apprehended together with its preevident proof, will be preevident, so that the argument is reversed and the proof probative of the nonevident is not found to be preevident. If, therefore, proof is neither apparent of the apparent, nor nonevident of the nonevident, nor nonevident of the preevident, nor preevident of the nonevident, and besides these, as they say, there is no other alternative, then we must declare that proof is nothing.

Furthermore, there is this also to be said. Proof **180** is a matter of controversy; for some declare that it does not even exist, as do those who assert that nothing at all exists,* but others, including the majority of the dogmatists, that it does exist; and we affirm that it is "no more" existent than nonexistent. And

181 besides, proof always contains a dogma, and they are in dispute about every dogma, so that there must necessarily be dispute about every proof. For if (for the sake of argument) when the proof for the existence of void is accepted the existence of void is likewise accepted, it is plain that those who dispute the existence of void dispute its proof also; and the same argument applies to all the other dogmas with which the proofs are concerned. Therefore every proof is questioned and is in dispute.

182 Since, then, proof is nonevident, owing to the controversy which exists concerning it (for things controverted, in so far as controverted, are nonevident), its existence is not self-evident but needs to be established for us by proof. The proof, then, by which proof is established will not be evident and agreed (for we are now inquiring whether proof in general exists), and being thus in dispute and nonevident it will need another proof, and this again a third, and so on *ad infinitum.* But it is impossible to prove an infinite series; therefore it is impossible to show that proof exists.

183 But neither can it be revealed by means of a sign. For since it is a matter of inquiry whether sign exists, and since the sign needs proof to ensure its reality, we find ourselves involved in circular reasoning—the proof requiring a sign, and the sign in turn

---

*I.e., is real, as opposed to phenomenal; so Xenophanes, Xeniades, and Gorgias.

a proof; which is absurd. And for these reasons neither is it possible to decide the controversy regarding proof, seeing that the decision requires a criterion, but—because it is a matter of inquiry, as we have shown, whether a criterion exists, and consequently the criterion needs a proof showing the existence of a criterion—we are again involved in the perplexity of circular reasoning. If, then, neither by proof nor by **184** sign nor by criterion it is possible to show that proof exists, and it is not evident of itself either, as we have shown, then it will be nonapprehensible whether proof exists. Consequently, proof will also be unreal; for it is conceived together with the act of proving, and were it not apprehended it would be unable to prove. Wherefore proof will not exist.

Thus much it will be enough to say by way of **185** outline and in criticism of proof. The dogmatists, however, maintaining the opposite view assert that the arguments propounded against proof are either probative or not probative; and if they are not probative, they are incapable of showing that proof does not exist; while if they are probative, they themselves involve the reality of proof by self-refutation. Hence also they **186** propound an argument in this form: "If proof exists, proof exists; if proof exists not, proof exists; but proof either exists or exists not; therefore proof exists." With the same intention they propound also this argument: "That which follows logically from contradictories is not only true but necessary; 'proof exists' and 'proof exists not' are contradictories, and the existence of proof follows from each of them; therefore proof exists."

187   Now to this we may reply, for instance, that, because we do not believe that any argument is probative, we do not assert either that the arguments against proof are absolutely probative but that they appear to us plausible; but those that are plausible are not necessarily probative. Yet if they actually are probative (which we do not positively affirm) they certainly are also true. And true arguments are those which deduce what is true by means of true premises; wherefore their inference is true. Now the inference was this—"therefore proof does not exist"; therefore the statement "proof does not exist" is true by re-

188 versing the argument. And just as purgative medicines expel themselves together with the substances already present in the body, so these arguments are capable of cancelling themselves along with the other arguments which are said to be probative. Nor is this preposterous, since in fact the saying "nothing is true" not only refutes every other saying but also nullifies itself as well.

And as regards this argument—"If proof exists, proof exists; and if proof does not exist, proof exists; but it either exists or exists not; therefore it exists"— there are a number of ways by which it can be shown to be inconclusive, but for the moment the following

189 method may suffice. If the hypothetical premise "If proof exists, proof exists" is valid, the contradictory of its consequent, namely "proof does not exist," must conflict with "proof exists," for this is the antecedent of the hypothetical premise. But, according to them, it is impossible for a hypothetical premise to be valid when composed of conflicting clauses. For the hypothetical premise promises that when its antecedent is true its consequent is also true, whereas conflicting clauses contrariwise promise that if either one of them is true the other cannot possibly be true. If therefore the premise "If proof exists, proof exists" is valid, the premise "If proof exists not, proof exists" cannot be valid. And again, conversely, if we grant by way **190** of assumption that the premise "If proof exists not, proof exists" is valid, then the clause "If proof exists" can coexist with "proof exists not." But if it can coexist with it, it is not in conflict with it. Therefore, in the premise "If proof exists, proof exists," the contrary of its consequent is not in conflict with its antecedent, so that, conversely, this premise will not be valid, as the former was posited, by agreement, as valid. And as the clause "proof exists not" is not in conflict **191** with "proof exists," the disjunctive "Either proof exists or proof exists not" will not be valid; for the valid disjunctive promises that one of its clauses is valid, but the other or others false and contradictory. Or else, if the disjunctive be valid, the hypothetical premise "If proof exists not, proof exists" is, in turn, found to be fallacious, as composed of conflicting clauses. So then the premises in the foregoing argument are discordant and mutually destructive; wherefore the argument is not valid. And further, **192** they are unable even to show that anything follows logically from the contradictories, since, as we have argued, they possess no criterion of logical consequence or deduction.

But this discussion is, in fact, superfluous. For if, on the one hand, the arguments in defense of proof are (let it be granted) plausible, while, on the other hand, the criticisms directed against proof are also plausible, then we must necessarily suspend judgment concerning proof also, and declare that proof is "no more" existent than nonexistent.

CHAPTER XIV. CONCERNING SYLLOGISMS

193 So then it is also superfluous, perhaps, to discuss in detail the much vaunted "syllogisms," since, for one thing, they are included in the refutation of the existence of "proof" (for it is plain that if this is nonexistent there is no place either for probative argument), and for another, we have implicitly contradicted them in our previous statements, when in discussing redundancy we mentioned a certain method by which it is possible to show that all the probative arguments of the Stoics and the Peripatetics are really

194 inconclusive. Yet perhaps it will not be amiss to go further and deal with them separately, especially since these thinkers pride themselves upon them. Now there is much that one can say by way of suggesting their unreality, but in an outline sketch it is sufficient to treat of them by the method which follows. And I will deal at present with the axiomatic arguments; for if these are destroyed all the rest of the arguments are overthrown as well, since it is from these that they derive the proof of their deductions.

195 Well then, the premise "Every man is an animal"

is established by induction from the particular instances; for from the fact that Socrates, who is a
man, is also an animal, and Plato likewise, and Dion
and each one of the particular instances, they think
it possible to assert that every man is an animal;
so that if even a single one of the particulars should
apparently conflict with the rest the universal premise
is not valid; thus, for example, when most animals
move the lower jaw, and only the crocodile the upper,
the premise "Every animal moves the lower jaw" is
not true. So whenever they argue "Every man is an **196**
animal, and Socrates is a man, therefore Socrates
is an animal," proposing to deduce from the universal
proposition "Every man is an animal" the particular
proposition "Socrates therefore is an animal," which
in fact goes (as we have mentioned) to establish by
way of induction the universal proposition, they fall
into the error of circular reasoning, since they are
establishing the universal proposition inductively by
means of each of the particulars and deducing the
particular proposition from the universal syllogistical-
ly. So likewise in the case of such an argument as **197**
"Socrates is a man, but no man is four-footed, therefore Socrates is not four-footed," by proposing to
establish the premise "No man is four-footed" by
induction from the particular instances while wishing
to deduce each several particular from the premise
"No man is four-footed," they become involved in
the perplexity of the circular fallacy.

And a similar criticism may be passed upon the **198**
rest of the "axiomatic" arguments, as they are called

by the Peripatetics; and also upon arguments in the form "If it is day, it is light." For the proposition "If it is day, it is light" is capable, they say, of proving that "it is light," and the clause "it is light" in conjunction with "it is day" serves to establish the proposition "If it is day, it is light." For the hypothetical premise stated above would not have been considered valid unless the constant coexistence of "it is light" with "it is day" had already been observed. 199 If, then, one has to apprehend beforehand that when there is day there certainly is light also, in order to construct the hypothetical premise "If it is day, it is light," while by means of this premise we deduce that when it is day it is light, the coexistence of the being of day and of night being proved (so far as depends on the axiomatic argument before us) by the premise "If it is day, it is light," and that premise in turn being established by the coexistence of the facts aforesaid,—in this case also the fallacy of circular reasoning overthrows the substance of the argument.

200 So likewise with an argument in the form "If it is day, it is light; but it is not light; therefore it is not day." For from the fact that we do not observe day without light the hypothetical premise "If it is day, it is light" might be considered to be valid; just as if, should day, let us suppose, at some time appear, without the appearance of light, the premise would be said to be false; but, so far as concerns the axiomatic argument aforesaid, the nonexistence of day when light is nonexistent is proved by the premise "If it is day, it is light," so that each of these statements

needs for its confirmation the secure grasp of the other in order thereby to become credible by means of circular reasoning. Moreover, from the fact that **201** some things are unable to coexist—take, for instance, if you like, day and night—both the conjunctive negation "Not day exists and night exists" and the disjunctive "Either day exists or night exists" might be considered to be valid. But they consider that their non-coexistence is established both by the negative of the conjunctive and by the disjunctive, arguing "Not day exists and night exists; but in fact night exists; day therefore exists not"; and "Either it is day or it is night; but in fact it is night; therefore it is not day," or "It is not night, therefore it is day." Whence we argue again that if for establishing the **202** disjunctive proposition and the negative of the conjunctive we require to apprehend beforehand the fact that the judgments they contain are incapable of coexistence, while they believe that they are deducing this incapacity for coexistence by means of both the disjunctive and the negative conjunctive, we involve ourselves in circular reasoning, seeing that we are unable either to give credence to the aforesaid premises without having apprehended the incapacity for coexistence of the judgments they contain, or to affirm positively that incapacity before concluding the syllogisms based on these premises. Consequently, as **203** we possess no principle on which to ground belief owing to the circular style of the argument, we shall declare that, so far as depends on these statements, neither the third nor the fourth nor the fifth of the "axiomatic" syllogisms possesses valid substance.

For the present, then, it will suffice to have said thus much concerning syllogisms.

Chapter XV. Concerning Induction

204 It is also easy, I consider, to set aside the method of induction. For, when they propose to establish the universal from the particulars by means of induction, they will effect this by a review either of all or of some of the particular instances. But if they review some, the induction will be insecure, since some of the particulars omitted in the induction may contravene the universal; while if they are to review all, they will be toiling at the impossible, since the particulars are infinite and indefinite. Thus on both grounds, as I think, the consequence is that induction is invalidated.

Chapter XVI. Concerning Definitions

205 Further, the dogmatists take great pride in their systematic treatment of definitions, which they include in the logical division of their philosophic system, as they call it. So come and let us now make a few observations on definitions.

Now while the dogmatists hold that definitions have many uses, you will probably find that these fall under two main heads which, as they say, include
206 all their necessary uses; for, as they explain, definitions

are necessary in all cases either for apprehension or for instruction. If, then, we shall show that they are of use for neither of these purposes, we shall, I think, bring to naught all the labor so vainly spent on them by the dogmatists.

So then, without preliminary, if, on the one hand, **207** the man who knows not the object of definition is unable to define the object unknown to him, while, on the other hand, the man who knows and proceeds to define has not apprehended the object from its definition but has put together his definition to fit the object already apprehended, then the definition is not necessary for the apprehension of objects. And since, if we propose to define absolutely all things, we shall define nothing, because of the regress *ad infinitum;* while if we allow that some things are apprehended even without definitions, we are declaring that definitions are not necessary for apprehension, seeing that we are able to apprehend all things apart from definitions in the same way as the undefined objects were apprehended,—then we shall **208** either define absolutely nothing or we shall declare that definitions are not necessary.

And for these reasons they are not necessary for instruction either, as we shall discover. For just as the man who first perceived the object perceived it apart from definition, so likewise the man who receives instruction about it can be instructed without definition. Moreover, they judge the definitions by **209** the objects defined and declare those definitions to be faulty which include any attributes not belonging either to all or to some of the objects defined. Hence, whenever one states that man is "a rational immortal animal" or "a rational mortal literary animal," whereas no man is immortal, and some are not literary, such 210 a definition they say is faulty. And it may be also that the definitions do not admit of judgment owing to the infinity of the particulars by which they ought to be judged; and consequently they will not convey apprehension and instruction regarding the objects whereby they are judged, which evidently have been known beforehand, if at all, and apprehended beforehand.

And how could it be other than absurd to assert that definitions are of use for apprehension or instruction or elucidation of any kind, when they involve 211 us in such a fog of uncertainty? Thus, for instance, to take a ridiculous case, suppose that one wished to ask someone whether he had met a man riding a horse and leading a dog and put the question in this form—"O rational mortal animal, receptive of intelligence and science, have you met with an animal capable of laughter, with broad nails and receptive of political science, with his (posterior) hemispheres seated on a mortal animal capable of neighing, and leading a four-footed animal capable of barking?"— how would one be otherwise than ridiculous, in thus reducing the man to speechlessness concerning so familiar an object because of one's definitions?

So then we must declare that, so far as we may 212 judge by this, the definition is useless, whether it be described as "a statement which by a brief reminder

166

brings us to a conception of the objects which underlie the terms,"—as is plain (is it not?) from what we have said just a moment ago,—or as "a statement declaratory of the essence," or what you like. For in fact, in their desire to propound a definition of the definition they plunge into an endless controversy which I now pass over, because of the plan of my present treatise, although it seems to overthrow definitions.

So what I have said about definitions is enough for the present.

CHAPTER XVII. CONCERNING DIVISION

Inasmuch as some of the dogmatists affirm that "dialec- **213** tic" is "a science dealing with syllogism, induction, definition, and division," and, after our arguments concerning the criterion and the sign and proof, we have already discussed syllogisms and induction as well as definitions, we deem that it will not be amiss to treat shortly of "division" also. Division then, as they allege, is effected in four ways; either a name, or word, is divided into its significations, or a whole into parts, or a genus into species, or a species into particulars. But it is probably easy to show that, on the contrary, in respect of none of these does a divisive science exist.

CHAPTER XVIII. CONCERNING THE DIVISION OF A NAME INTO THINGS SIGNIFIED

Now they at once assert that the sciences of natural **214** objects exist whereas those of conventional objects have no existence, and that with reason. For science claims to be a thing that is firm and invariable, but the conventional objects are easily liable to change and variation, because their character is altered by the shifting of the conventions which depend upon ourselves. Since, then, the significance of names is based on convention and not on nature (for otherwise all men, barbarians as well as Greeks, would understand all the things signified by the terms, besides the fact that it is in our power at any time to point out and signify the objects by any other names we may choose), how would it be possible for a science capable of dividing a name into its significations to exist? Or how could dialectic really be, as some imagine, a "science of things which signify and are signified"?

Chapter XIX. Concerning Whole and Part

215 Whole and part we shall discuss in what we call our physical treatise, but at present we have to deal with the so-called division of the whole into its parts. When a man says that the decad is being divided into one and two and three and four, the decad is not being divided into these. For as soon as its first part, say one, is subtracted—granting for the moment that this can be done—there no longer subsists the decad but the number nine, something quite different from the 216 decad. Hence the division and the subtraction of the other parts is not made from the decad but from some other numbers, and these vary with each subtraction.

Probably then it is impracticable to divide the whole into what are called its parts. For, in fact, if the whole is divided into parts, the parts ought to be comprised in the whole before the act of division, but probably they are not so comprised. Thus for example—to base our argument once more on the decad—they say that nine is certainly a part of the decad, since it is divided into one plus nine. But so likewise is the number eight, since it is divided into eight plus two; and so also are the numbers seven, six, five, four, three, two, and one. If then all these **217** numbers are included in the decad, and when added together with it make up fifty-five, then fifty-five is included in the number ten, which is absurd. Therefore neither are its so-called parts included in the decad nor can the decad be divided into them, as a whole into parts, since they are not even seen in it at all.

And the same objections will confront us in the **218** case of magnitudes also, supposing one would wish, for example, to divide the magnitude of ten cubits. Probably, then, it is not practicable to divide a whole into parts.

CHAPTER XX. OF GENERA AND SPECIES

There still remains, then, the subject of genera and **219** species, which we shall discuss more at large else-where,* but here we shall deal with them concisely. If, on the one hand, they† assert that genera and

---

*But no such discussion is to be found in the extant works of Sextus.
†I.e., the Stoics.

species are mental concepts, our criticisms of the "regent part" and of "presentation" refute them; whereas if they assign to them a substantiality of their own, how will they reply to this objection? If **220** the genera exist, either they are equal in number to the species or else there is one genus common to all the species which are said to belong to it. If, then, the genera are equal in number to the species, there will no longer be a common genus to be divided into the species; while if it shall be said that the genus exists as one in all species, then each species partakes of either the whole or a part of it. But it certainly does not partake of the whole; for it is impossible that what is one real object should be equally included in separate things in such a way as to appear as a whole in each of those things in which it is said to exist. And if it partakes of a part, then, in the first place, all the genus will not, as they suppose, accompany the species, nor will "man" be "an animal" but a part of an animal—he will be substance, for **221** example, but neither animate nor sensitive. Then, in the next place, all the species will be said to partake either of the same part of their genus or of different parts; but to partake of the same part is impossible for the reasons stated above; while if they partake of different parts, the species will be generically dissimilar one to another (which they will not admit), and each genus will be infinite because cut up into infinite sections (not into the species only but also into the particulars, since it is actually seen in these along with its species; for Dion* is said to be an animal as well as a man). But if these consequences are absurd, then not even by way of parts do the species partake of their genus, it being a unity.

If, then, each several species partakes neither of **222** the whole genus nor of a part of it, how can it be said that the one genus exists in all its parts so as to be actually divided into them? No one, probably, could make such a statement unless by concocting some imaginary entities,† which will be overturned, as the attacks of the skeptics show, by the unsettled disputes of the dogmatists themselves.

Furthermore, there is this to be said. The species **223** are of this kind or of that kind: the genera of these species either are of both this kind and that kind, or of this kind but not of that kind, or neither of this kind nor of that kind. When, for instance, of the "somethings" (or particulars) some are corporeal others incorporeal, and some true others false, and some (it may be) white others black, and some very large others very small, and so on with the rest, the genus "something" (to take it for the sake of argument), which some regard as the *summum genus,* will either be all these or some of them or none. **224** But if the "something," and the genus too, is absolutely none of them, the inquiry comes to an end. And if we should say that it is all of them, then, besides the impossibility of such a statement, each of the species and of the particulars wherein it exists will

*The stock name for a specimen of "man."
†The Platonic Ideas.

have to be all. For just as when the genus "animal" is, as they assert, "an animate sensitive substance," each of its species is said to be substance and animate and sensitive, so likewise if the genus is both corporeal and incorporeal and false and true and black, it may be, and white and very small and very large, and all the rest, each of the species and of the particulars will be all these—which is contrary to observation.

225 So this too is false. But if the genus is some of them only, the genus of these will not be the genus of the rest; if, for instance, the genus "something" is corporeal it will not be that of the incorporeal, and if the genus "animal" is rational it will not be that of the irrational, so that there is neither an incorporeal "something" nor an irrational animal, and so likewise with all other cases; and this is absurd. Therefore the genus cannot be either of both this and that kind, or of this kind but not of that, or of neither this kind nor that; and if this be so, neither does the genus exist at all.

And if one should say that the genus is potentially all things, we shall reply that what is potentially something must also be actually something, as, for instance, no one can be potentially literary without being so actually. So too, if the genus is potentially all things, what, we ask them, is it actually? And thus we find that the same difficulties remain. For it cannot

226 actually be all the contraries; nor yet can it be some of them actually and some only potentially—corporeal, for instance, actually and incorporeal potentially. For it is potentially that which it is capable

of really being actually, but that which is actually corporeal is incapable of becoming incorporeal in actuality, so that if, for example, the genus "something" is actually corporeal it is not potentially incorporeal, and *vice versa.* It is impossible, therefore, for the genus to be some things actually and some only potentially. But if it is absolutely nothing actually, it has no substantial existence. Hence the genus, which they say they divide into the species, is nothing.

And further, here is another point worthy of **227** notice. Just as, because Alexander and Paris* are identical, it is impossible that the statement "Alexander walks" should be true when "Paris walks" is false, so also if "manhood" is identical for both Theon and Dion, the term "man" when introduced as an element in a judgment will cause the judgment to be equally true or false in the case of both. But this is not what we find; for when Dion is sitting and Theon walking, the judgment "man walks" is true when used of the one, but false of the other. Therefore the term "man" is not common to them both and the same for both but, if applicable at all, it is peculiar to one of the two.

CHAPTER XXI. CONCERNING COMMON PROPERTIES

Similar arguments apply also to the "common prop- **228** erties." For if vision is one and the same property in Dion and in Theon, then, suppose that Dion should

---

*Two names of the son of Priam who carried off Helen to Troy.

perish and Theon survive and retain his sight, either they will assert that the vision of the perished Dion remains unperished, which is incredible, or they will declare that the same vision has both perished and not perished, which is absurd; therefore the vision of Theon is not identical with Dion's but, if anything, the vision of each is peculiar to himself. And if breathing is an identical property in Dion and Theon, it is impossible that breathing should exist in Theon and not exist in Dion; but this is possible when the one has perished and the other survives; therefore it is not identical.

However, as regards this subject, this concise statement will be sufficient for the present.

Chapter XXII. Concerning Sophisms

229 It will not, perhaps, be amiss to give our attention for a moment to the subject of sophisms, seeing that those who glorify dialectic declare that it is indispensable for exposing sophisms. For, they say, if dialectic is capable of distinguishing true and false arguments, and sophisms are false arguments, it will also be capable of discerning these, which distort the truth by apparent plausibilities. Hence the dialecticians, by way of assisting life when it totters, strive earnestly to teach us the conception of sophisms, their differences and their solutions. They declare that a sophism is "a plausible argument cunningly framed to induce acceptance of the inference, it being either false or resembling what is false or nonevident or

otherwise unacceptable." It is false, for example, in **230** the case of the sophism "Nobody offers one a predicate to drink; but 'to drink absinth' is a predicate; nobody therefore offers one absinth to drink." Or again, it may resemble the false, as in this case—"What neither was nor is possible is not absurd; but it neither was nor is possible for a doctor, *qua* doctor, to murder; therefore it is not absurd that a doctor, *qua* doctor, should murder." Or again, it may be nonevident, as **231** thus—"It is not true both that I have asked you a question first and that the stars are not even in number; but I have asked you a question first; therefore the stars are even." Or again, it may be otherwise unacceptable, like the so-called solecistic arguments, such as—"That at which you look exists; but you have a frenzied look; therefore 'frenzied' exists; or "What you gaze at exists; but you gaze at an inflamed spot; therefore 'at an inflamed spot' exists."

Moreover, they attempt also to set forth solutions **232** of the sophisms, saying in the case of the first sophism that one thing is established by the premises and another inferred in the conclusion. For it is established that a predicate is not drunk and that "to drink absinth" is a predicate, but not "absinth" by itself. Hence, whereas one ought to infer "Nobody therefore drinks the 'to drink absinth,' " which is true, the inference drawn is "Nobody therefore drinks absinth," which is false, as not deduced from the established premises. And as regards the second sophism, they **233** explain that while it seems to lead in a false direction, so that it makes the inattentive hesitate in assenting to it, its conclusion is true, namely "It is not therefore absurd that the doctor, *qua* doctor, should murder." For no judgment is absurd, and "the doctor, *qua* doctor, murders" is a judgment, so that neither is

234 it absurd. And the method of leading up to the non-evident deals, they say, with the class of things that are variable.* For when, according to the assumption, no previous question has been asked, the negation of the conjunctive premise is true, the conjunctive or major premise being false because of its inclusion of the false clause "I have asked you a question first." But after the negation of the major has been asked, as the minor premise "I have asked you a question first" has become true, owing to the fact that the negation of the major has been asked before the minor premise, the first clause in the negation of the major becomes false while the false clause in the major has become true; so that it is never possible for the conclusion to be deduced if the negation of the major premise does not coexist with the minor premise.

235 And as to the last class—the solecistic arguments—some declare that they are introduced absurdly, contrary to linguistic usage.

Such are the statements made by some of the dialecticians concerning sophisms—though others indeed make other statements; and what they say may be able, perhaps, to tickle the ears of the casual hearer, superfluous though it is and the result of vain labor on their part. Probably this can be seen from what

---

*I.e., judgments which change from truth to falsehood.

we have said already; for we have shown that truth and falsehood, according to the dialecticians, cannot be apprehended, and that by a variety of arguments as well as by the refutation of their evidences for the validity of the syllogism, namely proof and axiomatic arguments. And there are many other special **236** objections bearing on the topic before us which we might mention, but now, for brevity's sake, we mention only this one.

As regards all the sophisms which dialectic seems peculiarly able to expose, their exposure is useless; whereas in all cases where exposure is useful, it is not the dialectician who will expose them but the experts in each particular art who grasp the connection of the facts. Thus, for instance, to mention **237** one or two examples, if a sophism such as this were propounded—"In diseases, at the stages of abatement, a varied diet and wine are to be approved; but in every type of disease an abatement inevitably occurs before the first third day*; it is necessary, therefore, to take for the most part a varied diet and wine before the first third day,"—in this case the dialectician would be unable to assist in exposing the argument, useful though the exposure would be, but the doctor will expose the sophism, since he knows that the **238** term "abatement" is used in two senses, of the general "abatement" in the disease and of the tendency to betterment after the crisis in the strained local con-

---

*The "methodic" school of medicine held that the progress of a disease was marked by three-day periods of increasing (up to the crisis) or decreasing severity; for the former they prescribed a light diet.

ditions, and this improvement in the local strain generally occurs before the first third day, but it is not for this but for the general abatement in the disease that we recommend the varied diet. Consequently he will say that the premises are discordant, since one kind of "abatement" is adopted in the first premise, namely that of the general condition, and another—that of the local condition—in the second premise.

239   Again, in the case of one who suffers from fever due to aggravated "contraction" or obstruction, if an argument is propounded in the form—"Opposites are cures of opposites; cold is the opposite of the present feverish condition; therefore cold is the treatment which corresponds to the present feverish condition,"—here again the dialectician will keep silence, **240** but the doctor, since he knows what morbid states are fundamentally persistent and what are symptoms of such states, will declare that the argument does not apply to the symptoms (not to mention the fact that the result of the application of cold is to aggravate the feverish condition) but to the persistent morbid states, and that the constipation is persistent but requires an expansive method of treatment rather than contraction, whereas the resultant symptom of inflammation is not fundamentally persistent, nor (consequently) is the state of cold which seems to correspond thereto.

241   Thus, as regards sophisms the exposure of which is useful, the dialectician will not have a word to say, but he will propound for us such arguments as these—"If it is not so that you both have fair horns and have horns, you have horns; but it is not so that you have fair horns and have horns; therefore you have horns." "If a thing moves, it moves either **242** in the spot where it is or where it is not; but it moves neither in the spot where it is (for it is at rest) nor in that where it is not (for how could a thing be active in a spot where it does not so much as exist?); therefore nothing moves." "Either the existent be- **243** comes or the nonexistent; now the existent does not become (for it exists); nor yet does the nonexistent (for the becoming is passive but the nonexistent is not passive); therefore nothing becomes." "Snow is frozen water; but water is black; therefore snow is **244** black."

And when he has made a collection of such trash he draws his eyebrows together, and expounds dialectic and endeavors very solemnly to establish for us by syllogistic proofs that a thing becomes, a thing moves, snow is white, and we do not have horns, although it is probably sufficient to confront the trash with the plain fact in order to smash up their positive affirmation by means of the equipollent contradictory evidence derived from appearances. Thus, in fact, a certain philosopher,* when the argument against motion was put to him, without a word started to walk about; and people who follow the usual way of life proceed on journeys by land and sea and build ships and houses and beget children

---

*Diogenes the Cynic.

245   without paying any attention to the arguments against motion and becoming. And we are told of an amusing retort made by the physician Herophilus*: he was a contemporary of Diodorus who, being given to juggling with dialectic, used to promulgate sophistical arguments against motion as well as many other things. So when Diodorus had dislocated his shoulder he came to Herophilus to get treated, and the latter jestingly said to him—"Your shoulder has been put out either in the place where it was or where it was not; but it was put out neither where it was nor where it was not; therefore it has not been put out"; so that the sophist begged him to leave such arguments alone and apply the treatment prescribed by medical

246   art as suitable to his case. For it is, I think, sufficient to conduct one's life empirically and undogmatically in accordance with the rules and beliefs that are commonly accepted, suspending judgment regarding the statements derived from dogmatic subtlety and furthest removed from the usage of life. If, then, dialectic would fail to expose any of the sophisms which might usefully be exposed, while the exposure of all the sophisms which we might perhaps grant it capable of exposing are useless, then in respect of the exposure of sophisms dialectic is useless.

247   Starting even from the actual statements made by the dialecticians one might show concisely in this wise that their technical arguments about sophisms are superfluous. The dialecticians assert that they have

---

*A famous anatomist at Cos, ca. 300 B.C.

resorted to the art of dialectic not simply for the sake of ascertaining what is deduced from what but chiefly for the sake of knowing how to discern the true and the false by means of probative arguments. Thus they declare that dialectic is "the science of what is true and false and neither." Since, then, they assert **248** that a true argument is one which draws a true conclusion by means of true premises, when an argument is propounded which has a false conclusion we shall at once know that it is false and shall not yield it assent. For the argument itself must either be illogical or contain premises that are not true. The following **249** considerations show this clearly: The false conclusion in the argument either follows from the combination formed by its premises, or it does not so follow. But if it does so follow, neither will the argument be logically sound; for an argument, they say, is logically sound when its conclusion follows from the combination formed by its premises. If, again, it does so follow, then—according to their own technical treatises—the combination formed by its premises must necessarily be false; for they say that the false follows from the false and nohow from the true. And from what we have already said it is plain that ac- **250** cording to them the argument which is not logically sound or not true is not probative either.

If, then, when an argument is propounded with a false conclusion we know at once that the argument is neither true nor logically sound, because of its false conclusion, we shall not assent to it, even if we fail to see wherein the fallacy lies. For just as we refuse our assent to the truth of the tricks performed by jugglers and know that they are deluding us, even if we do not know how they do it, so likewise we refuse to believe arguments which, though seemingly plausible, are false, even when we do not know how they are fallacious.

251 Further, since the sophism leads, they say, not only to falsehood but also to other absurdities, we must discuss it more at large. The argument propounded leads us either to an inadmissible conclusion or to one of such a sort that we must needs admit it. In the latter case we shall assent to it without absurdity; but if it leads to what is inadmissible, it is not we that ought to yield hasty assent to the absurdity because of its plausibility, but it is they that ought to abstain from the argument which constrains them to assent to absurdities, if they really choose to seek truth, as they profess, rather than **252** drivel like children. Thus, suppose there were a road leading up to a chasm, we do not push ourselves into the chasm just because there is a road leading to it but we avoid the road because of the chasm; so, in the same way, if there should be an argument which leads us to a confessedly absurd conclusion, we shall not assent to the absurdity just because of the argument but avoid the argument because of the **253** absurdity. So whenever such an argument is propounded to us we shall suspend judgment regarding each premise, and when finally the whole argument is propounded we shall draw what conclusions we approve.

And if the dogmatists of the school of Chrysippus declare that when the "sorites"* is being propounded they ought to halt while the argument is still proceeding and suspend judgment, to avoid falling into absurdity, much more, surely, would it be fitting for us, who are skeptics, when we suspect absurdity, to give no hasty approval of the premises propounded but rather to suspend judgment about each until the completion of the whole series which forms the argument. And whereas we, by starting undogmatically **254** from the observation of practical life, thus avoid these fallacious arguments, the dogmatists will not be in a position to distinguish the sophism from the argument which seems to be correctly propounded, seeing that they have to pronounce dogmatically that the form of the argument is, or is not, logically sound and also that the premises are, or are not, true. For we have shown above that they are neither able to **255** apprehend the logically valid arguments nor yet capable of deciding that a thing is true, since—as we have shown from their own statements—they possess neither a criterion nor a demonstration that commands general agreement. Thus far, then, the technical treatment of sophisms so much talked of amongst the dialecticians is otiose.

And we say much the same regarding the distinguishing of ambiguities. For if the ambiguity is **256**

---

*The fallacy of the "heap," so called because commonly framed thus: "There is a heap of grain: Take away one grain—two grains—three grains, and so on. Is it still a heap?" In modern logic "sorites" denotes a chain of syllogisms in which all the conclusions save the last are suppressed.

a word or phrase having two or more meanings, and it is by convention that words have meanings, then all such ambiguities as can be usefully cleared up—such, that is, as occur in the course of some practical affair—will be cleared up, not certainly by the dialectician, but by the craftsmen trained in each several art, as they have personal experience of the conventional way adopted by themselves of using the
257 terms to denote the objects signified—as, for example, in the ambiguity "In periods of abatement one should sanction a varied diet and wine." And in the ordinary affairs of life we see already how people—ay, and even the slave boys—distinguish ambiguities when they think such distinction is of use. Certainly, if a master who had servants named alike were to bid a boy called, say, "Manes" (supposing this to be a common name for a servant) to be summoned, the slave boy will ask "Which one?" And if a man who had several different wines were to say to his boy "Pour me out a draught of wine," then too the boy
258 will ask "Which one?" Thus it is the experience of what is useful in each affair that brings about the distinguishing of ambiguities.

All such ambiguities, however, as are not involved in the practical experiences of life but in dogmatic opinions, and are no doubt useless for a life void of dogmatism,—concerning these the dialectician, in his own peculiar position, will be similarly forced, in view of the skeptic attacks, to suspend judgment, in so far as they are probably linked up with matters that are nonevident and nonappre-

hensible, or even nonsubstantial. This subject, how- **259**
ever, we shall discuss later on; and if any dogmatist
should attempt to refute any of our statements he
will be strengthening the skeptic argument by adding
support to their suspension of judgment about the
matters in question as a result of our mutual an-
tagonism and interminable dissention.

Having said thus much concerning ambiguities
we now conclude therewith our second book of
"Outlines."

BOOK III

1 Concerning the logical division of what is called "philosophy" the foregoing account may suffice by way of outline.

CHAPTER I. OF THE PHYSICAL DIVISION

Pursuing the same method of exposition in our investigation of the physical division of philosophy, we shall not refute each of their statements in order, but we shall endeavor to overthrow those of a more general character wherein the rest also are included.

Let us begin with their doctrine of principles.

CHAPTER II. OF EFFICIENT PRINCIPLES

Since it is agreed by most that of principles some are material and some efficient, we shall make our argument start with the efficient; for these, as they assert, are superior to the material.

CHAPTER III. CONCERNING GOD

2 Since, then, the majority have declared that God is a most efficient cause, let us begin by inquiring about

God, first premising that although, following the
ordinary view, we affirm undogmatically that gods
exist and reverence gods and ascribe to them fore-
knowledge, yet as against the rashness of the dogmatists we argue as follows.

When we conceive objects we ought to form
conceptions of their substances as well, as, for instance, whether they are corporeal or incorporeal.
And also of their forms; for no one could conceive
"horse" unless he had first learned the horse's form.
And of course the object conceived must be conceived
as existing somewhere. Since, then, some of the dog-   **3**
matists assert that God is corporeal, others that he
is incorporeal, and some that he has human form,
others not, and some that he exists in space, others
not; and of those who assert that he is in space some
put him inside the world, others outside; how shall
we be able to reach a conception of God when we
have no agreement about his substance or his form
or his place of abode? Let them first agree and consent
together that God is of such and such a nature, and
then, when they have sketched out for us that nature,
let them require that we should form a conception
of God. But so long as they disagree interminably,
we cannot say what agreed notion we are to derive
from them.

But, say they,* when you have conceived of a   **4**
being imperishable and blessed, regard this as God.
But this is foolish; for just as one who does not know

---

*I.e., the Stoics and Epicurus.

Dion is unable also to conceive the properties which belong to him as Dion, so also when we do not know the substance of God we shall also be unable

5 to learn and conceive his properties. And apart from this, let them tell us what a "blessed" thing is—whether it is that which energizes according to virtue and foreknows what is subject to itself, or that which is void of energy and neither performs any work itself nor provides work for another. For indeed about this also they disagree interminably and thus render "the blessed" something we cannot conceive, and therefore God also.

6 Further, in order to form a conception of God one must necessarily—so far as depends on the dogmatists—suspend judgment as to his existence or nonexistence. For the existence of God is not pre-evident.* For if God impressed us automatically, the dogmatists would have agreed together regarding his essence, his character, and his place; whereas their interminable disagreement has made him seem to us

7 nonevident and needing demonstration. Now he that demonstrates the existence of God does so by means of what is either preevident or nonevident. Certainly not, then, by means of the preevident; for if what demonstrates God's existence were preevident, then—since the thing proved is conceived together with that which proves it, and therefore is apprehended along with it as well, as we have established—God's existence also will be preevident, it being apprehended

---

*Plainly manifest, self-evident.

188

along with the preevident fact which proves it. But, as we have shown, it is not preevident; therefore it is not proved, either, by a preevident fact. Nor yet by what is nonevident. For if the nonevident fact **8** which is capable of proving God's existence, needing proof as it does, shall be said to be proved by means of a preevident fact, it will no longer be nonevident but preevident. Therefore the nonevident fact which proves his existence is not proved by what is preevident. Nor yet by what is nonevident; for he who asserts this will be driven into circular reasoning when we keep demanding proof every time for the nonevident fact which he produces as proof of the last one propounded. Consequently, the existence of God cannot be proved from any other fact. But if God's **9** existence is neither automatically preevident nor proved from another fact, it will be inapprehensible.

There is this also to be said. He who affirms that God exists either declares that he has, or that he has not, forethought for the things in the universe, and in the former case that such forethought is for all things or for some things. But if he had forethought for all, there would have been nothing bad and no badness in the world; yet all things, they say, are full of badness; hence it shall not be said that God forethinks all things. If, again, he forethinks some, **10** why does he forethink these things and not those? For either he has both the will and the power to forethink all things, or else he has the will but not the power, or the power but not the will, or neither the will nor the power. But if he had had both the will and the power he would have had forethought for all things; but for the reasons stated above he does not forethink all; therefore he has not both the will and the power to forethink all. And if he has the will but not the power, he is less strong than the cause which renders him unable to forethink what **11** he does not forethink: but it is contrary to our notion of God that he should be weaker than anything. And if, again, he has the power but not the will to have forethought for all, he will be held to be malignant; while if he has neither the will nor the power, he is both malignant and weak—an impious thing to say about God. Therefore God has no forethought for the things in the universe.

But if he exercises no forethought for anything, and there exists no work nor product of his, no one will be able to name the source of the apprehension of God's existence, inasmuch as he neither appears of himself nor is apprehended by means of any of his products. So for these reasons we cannot appre- **12** hend whether God exists. And from this we further conclude that those who positively affirm God's existence are probably compelled to be guilty of im- piety; for if they say that he forethinks all things they will be declaring that God is the cause of what is evil, while if they say that he forethinks some things or nothing they will be forced to say that God is either malignant or weak, and obviously this is to use impious language.

Chapter IV. Concerning Cause

To prevent the dogmatists attempting also to slander **13** us, because of their inability to refute us in a practical way, we shall discuss the question of the efficient cause more at large when we have first tried to give attention to the conception of cause. Now so far as the statements of the dogmatists are concerned, it would be impossible for anyone even to conceive cause, since, in addition to offering discrepant and contradictory conceptions of cause, they have rendered its substance also indiscoverable by their disagreement about it. For some affirm cause to be **14** corporeal, others incorporeal. In the broad sense, a cause would seem to be, according to them, "that by whose energizing the effect comes about"; as, for example, the sun or the sun's heat is the cause of the wax being melted or of the melting of the wax. For even on this point they are at variance, some declaring that cause is causal of nouns, such as "the melting," others of predicates, such as "being melted." Hence, as I said, in the broad sense cause will be "that by whose energizing the effect comes about."

The majority of them hold that of these causes **15** some are immediate, some associate, some cooperant; and that causes are "immediate" when their presence involves the presence, and their removal the removal, and their decrease the decrease, of the effect (it is thus, they say, that the fixing on of the halter causes the strangling); and that an "associate" cause is one which contributes a force equal to that of its fellow cause towards the production of the effect (it is thus, they say, that each of the oxen which draw the plow is a cause of the drawing of the plow); and that a "cooperant" cause is one which contributes a slight force towards the easy production of the effect, as in the case when two men are lifting a heavy load with difficulty the assistance of a third helps to lighten it.

16 Some of them, however, have asserted further that things present are causes of things future, being "antecedents"; as when intense exposure to the sun causes fever. But this view is rejected by some, on the ground that, since the cause is relative to something existent and to a real effect, it cannot precede it as its cause.

As regards this controversy, our position is as follows:

CHAPTER V. DOES ANYTHING CAUSE ANYTHING?

17 That Cause* exists is plausible; for how could there come about increase, decrease, generation, corruption, motion in general, each of the physical and mental effects, the ordering of the whole universe, and everything else, except by reason of some cause? For even if none of these things has real existence, we shall affirm that it is due to some cause that

---

*To mark the distinction between [the Greek] *aition* and *aitia,* I render the former by "Cause," the latter by "cause." The latter seems used mostly of the particular instance, the former of the general notion; or the former of the cause of existence, the latter of the cause of cognition.

they appear to us other than they really are. Moreover, **18** if cause were nonexistent everything would have been produced by everything and at random. Horses, for instance, might be born, perchance, of flies, and elephants of ants; and there would have been severe rains and snow in Egyptian Thebes, while the southern districts would have had no rain, unless there had been a cause which makes the southern parts stormy, the eastern dry. Also, he who asserts that there is **19** no Cause is refuted; for if he says that he makes this assertion absolutely and without any cause, he will not win credence; but if he says that he makes it owing to some cause, he is positing Cause while wishing to abolish it, since he offers us a cause to prove the nonexistence of Cause.

For these reasons, then, the existence of Cause is plausible. But that it is also plausible to say that **20** nothing is the Cause of anything will be evident when we have set forth, to suit the occasion, a few of the many arguments which go to prove this case. Thus it is, for example, impossible to conceive the Cause before apprehending its effect as *its* effect; for we only recognize that it is causative of the effect when we apprehend the latter as an effect. But we cannot **21** either apprehend the effect of the Cause as *its* effect unless we apprehend the Cause of the effect as *its* Cause; for we think we know that it is its effect only when we have apprehended the Cause of it as its Cause. If, then, in order to conceive the Cause, we **22** must first know the effect, while in order to know the effect we must, as I said, have previous knowledge of the Cause, the fallacy of this circular mode of reasoning proves both to be inconceivable, the Cause being incapable of being conceived as the Cause, and the effect as effect. For since each of them needs the evidence of the other, we shall not be able to say which conception is to have the precedence. Hence we shall be unable to declare that anything is the Cause of anything.

23   And even were one to grant that Cause can be conceived, it might be held to be inapprehensible because of the divergency of opinion. For he who says that there is some Cause of something either asserts that he makes this statement absolutely and without basing it on any rational cause, or else he will declare that he has arrived at his conviction owing to certain causes. If, then, he says that he states it "absolutely," he will be no more worthy of credence than the man who asserts "absolutely" that nothing is a cause of anything; whereas if he shall mention causes on account of which he holds that something causes something, he will be attempting to support the matter in question by means of that matter itself; for when we are examining the question whether anything is the Cause of anything, he asserts that Cause exists since there exists a cause for the existence **24** of Cause. Besides, since we are inquiring about the reality of Cause, it will certainly be necessary for him to produce a cause for the cause of the existence of Cause, and of that cause yet another, and so on *ad infinitum.* But it is impossible to produce causes infinite in number. It is impossible, therefore, to affirm positively that anything is Cause of anything.

Moreover, the Cause, when it produces the effect, **25** either is and subsists already as causal or is non-causal. Certainly it is not noncausal; while if it is causal, it must first have subsisted and become causal, and thereafter produces the effect which is said to be brought about by it as already existing Cause. But since the Cause is relative and relative to the effect, it is clear that it cannot be prior in existence to the latter; therefore not even as being causal can the Cause bring about that whereof it is Cause. And if it does not bring about anything either as being **26** or as not being causal, then it does not bring anything about; and hence it will not be a Cause; for apart from its effecting something the Cause cannot be conceived as Cause.

Hence some people argue thus: The Cause must either subsist along with its effect or before it or must come into being after it. Now to say that the Cause is brought into existence after the appearance of its effect would seem ridiculous. But neither can it subsist before the effect; for it is said to be conceived in relation thereto, and they affirm that relatives, in so **27** far as they are relative, coexist with each other and are conceived together. Nor, again, can it subsist along with its effect; for if it is productive of the effect, and what comes into existence must so come by the agency of what exists already, the Cause must have become causal first, and this done, then produces its effect. If, then, the Cause neither subsists before its effect, nor subsists along with it, nor does the effect precede the Cause, it would seem that it has

28 no substantial existence at all. And it is clear probably that by these arguments the conception of Cause is overthrown again. For if Cause as a relative notion cannot be conceived before its effect, and yet, if it is to be conceived as causative of its effect, it must be conceived before its effect, while it is impossible for anything to be conceived before that which the conception of it cannot precede,—then it is impossible for the Cause to be conceived.

29 From this we conclude finally that—if the arguments by which it was shown that we ought to affirm the existence of Cause are plausible, and if the arguments which go to prove that it is improper to declare that any Cause exists are likewise plausible, and if it is inadmissible to prefer any of these arguments to the others, since, as we have shown above, we confessedly possess neither sign nor criterion nor proof,—we are compelled to suspend judgment concerning the real existence of Cause, declaring that a Cause is "no more" existent than nonexistent, if we are to judge by the statements made by the dogmatists.

CHAPTER VI. CONCERNING MATERIAL PRINCIPLES

30 So far, then, as concerns the efficient principle this account will suffice for the present. But we must also give a brief account of what are called the material principles. Now that these are inapprehensible may easily be gathered from the disagreement which exists about them amongst the dogmatists. For Pherecydes of Syros* declared earth to be the principle of all things; Thales of Miletus,† water; Anaximander (his pupil), the unlimited; Anaximenes and Diogenes of Apollonia, air; Hippasus of Metapontum, fire; Xenophanes of Colophon, earth and water; Oenopides of Chios, fire and air; Hippo of Rhegium, fire and water; Onomacritus, in his *Orphica,* fire and water and earth; 31 the school of Empedocles as well as the Stoics, fire, air, water, and earth—for why should one even mention that mysterious "indeterminate matter" which some of them talk about, when not even they themselves are positive that they apprehend it? Aristotle the Peripatetic takes as his principles fire, air, water, earth, and the "revolving body"‡; Democritus and 32 Epicurus, atoms; Anaxogoras of Clazomenae, homeomeries§; Diodorus, surnamed Cronos, minimal and noncomposite bodies; Heracleides Ponticus** and Asclepiades the Bithynian,†† homogeneous masses; the school of Pythagoras,‡‡ the numbers;

---

*[Fl. ca. 550 B.C. Mythologist and cosmologist.]

†[Thales, Anaximander, Anaximenes, Diogenes, Hippasus, Oenopides, and Hippo were natural philosophers of the sixth and fifth centuries B.C.; Onomacritus was a sixth-century B.C. Athenian religious poet; Empedocles (ca. 493–433 B.C.) denied the unity and immobility of Parmenidean matter. For Parmenides, see Book III, chapter 10.]

‡[The fifth element, the ether, or upper atmosphere.]

§"Things with like parts" or homogeneous substances.

**[Ca. 390–322 B.C. Greek philosopher and astronomer.]

††[First-century B.C. physician at Rome.]

‡‡[Ca. 580–500 B.C. He is said to have discovered the numerical ratios determining the principal intervals of the musical scale, from which he interpreted the world as a whole through numbers.]

the mathematicians, the limits of bodies; Strato the physicist,* the qualities.

33   Since, then, there exists amongst them as much divergence as this, and even more, regarding the material principles, we shall give assent either to all the positions stated, and all others as well, or to some of them. But to assent to all is not possible; for we certainly shall not be able to assent both to Asclepiades, who says that the elements can be broken up and possess qualities, and to Democritus, who asserts that they are indivisible and void of quality, and to Anaxagoras, who leaves every sensible quality at-

34 tached to the homeomeries. Yet if we shall prefer any one standpoint, or view, to the rest, we shall be preferring it either absolutely and without proof or with proof. Now without proof we shall not yield assent; and if it is to be with proof, the proof must be true. But a true proof can only be given when approved by a true criterion, and a criterion is shown

35 to be true by means of an approved proof. If, then, in order to show the truth of the proof which prefers any one view, its criterion must be proved, and to prove the criterion in turn its proof must be pre-established, the argument is found to be the circular one which will not allow the reasoning to go forward, since the proof keeps always requiring a proved

---

*[D. ca. 270 B.C. Peripatetic philosopher who showed that the Democritean "empty space" does not exist as a "continuum" under natural conditions, but only as discontinuous intermittent reality within bodies. Whenever a continuous empty space is created by artificial conditions, the molecular parts of the body try to close it at once. For Democritus, see Book I, chapter 30.]

criterion, and the criterion an approved proof. And **36** should any one propose to approve the criterion by a criterion and to prove the proof by a proof, he will be driven to a regress *ad infinitum*. Accordingly, if we are unable to assent either to all the views held about the elements or to any one of them, it is proper to suspend judgment about them.

Now though it is, perhaps, possible to show by **37** these arguments alone the inapprehensibility of the elements and of the material principles, yet in order that we may be able to refute the dogmatists in a more comprehensive manner we shall dwell on this topic at appropriate length. And since the opinions about the elements are, as we have shown, numerous and well-nigh infinite, we will excuse ourselves— because of the character of our present treatise—from discussing each opinion in detail, but will make answer to them all implicitly. For since the elements, whatever view one takes of them, must be finally regarded either as corporeal or incorporeal, we think it enough to show that corporeal things are inapprehensible and incorporeal things inapprehensible; for thus it will be clear that the elements are also inapprehensible.

CHAPTER VII. ARE BODIES APPREHENSIBLE?

Some say that body is that which is capable of being **38** active or passive. But so far as this conception goes it is inapprehensible. For, as we have shown, Cause is inapprehensible; and if we cannot say whether any Cause exists, neither can we say whether anything passive exists; for what is passive is certainly made passive by a Cause. And when both the Cause and the passive object are inapprehensible, the result will be that body also is inapprehensible. But some define **39** body as what has three dimensions combined with resistance or solidity. For they describe the point as that which has no parts, the line as length without breadth, the surface as length with breadth; and when this takes on both depth and resistance there is formed body—the object of our present discussion—it being composed of length and breadth and depth and re- **40** sistance. The answer, however, to these people is simple. For they will say either that body is nothing more than these qualities, or that it is something else than the combination of the qualities already mentioned. Now apart from length and breadth and depth and solidity the body would be nothing; but if these things are the body, anyone who shall prove that they are unreal will likewise abolish the body; for wholes are abolished along with the sum of their parts.

Now it is possible to disprove these dimensions in a variety of ways; but for the present it will be enough to say that if the limits exist, they are either **41** lines or surfaces or bodies. If, then, one should affirm the existence of a surface or a line, then it will be affirmed that each of the aforementioned objects either can exist of itself or is cognized solely in connection with so-called bodies. But to imagine either a line or a surface as existing of itself is doubtless silly. While if it should be said that each of these objects is cognized solely in connection with the bodies and has no independent existence, it will thereby be granted, in the first place, that the bodies are not generated from them (for if so, I suppose, these objects ought to have had independent existence first, and then have combined to form the bodies); and further, they have **42** no real existence even in the so-called bodies.

This can be shown by several arguments, but for the present it will suffice to mention the difficulties which arise from the fact of touch. For if juxtaposed bodies touch one another they are in contact with their limits—for example, with their surfaces. The surfaces, then, will not be completely unified one with another as a result of touching, since otherwise touch would be fusion and the separation of things touching a rending apart; and this is not what we find. And if **43** the surface touches the surface of the juxtaposed body with some of its parts, and with other parts is united with the body of which it is a limit, it will not be without depth, since its parts are conceived as different in respect of depth, one part touching the juxtaposed body, the other being that which effects its union with the body whereof it is a limit. Hence, even in connection with body one cannot imagine length and breadth without depth, nor, consequently, surface.

So likewise when two surfaces are, let us imagine, juxtaposed along the limits where they come to an end, by way of what is called their "length," that is to say by way of their "lines," then these lines, by means of which the surfaces are said to touch each other, will not be unified (else they would be fused together); yet if each of them touches the line which lies next to it breadthwise with some of its parts and by others is united with the surface of which it is a limit, it will not be without breadth, and, consequently, it will not be a line. But if there exists in body neither line nor surface, neither length nor breadth nor depth will exist in body.

44 And should anyone assert that the limits are bodies, he can be answered very shortly. For if length is a body, it must needs be divided into its three dimensions, and each of these, in turn, being a body will be divided into three other dimensions, which will be bodies, and these likewise into others, and so on *ad infinitum,* so that the body comes to be of infinite size, being divided into an infinity of parts: this result is absurd, and therefore the dimensions aforesaid are not bodies. But if they are neither bodies nor lines nor surfaces, they will be held to have no existence.

45 Solidity also is inapprehensible. For if it is apprehended, it must be apprehended by touch. If, then, we shall prove that touch is inapprehensible, it will be clear that it is impossible for solidity to be apprehended. That touch is inapprehensible we argue as follows. Things which touch one another either touch with their parts or as wholes touching wholes. Now they certainly will not touch as wholes; for then they will be unified instead of being in contact with one another. Nor yet through parts touching parts; for their parts, though in relation to the wholes they are parts, are wholes in relation to their parts. So **46** these wholes, which are parts of other things, will not touch as wholes touching wholes, for the reasons aforesaid, nor yet through parts touching parts; for their parts, too, being wholes relatively to their own parts, will not be in contact either as wholes with wholes or as parts with parts. But if we apprehend the occurrence of touch neither by way of wholeness nor by way of parts, touch will be inapprehensible. And, consequently, solidity also; and, therefore, body; for if this is nothing more than the three dimensions *plus* solidity, and we have proved that each of these is inapprehensible, body also will be inapprehensible.

Thus, then, if we are to judge by the conception of body, it is inapprehensible whether any body exists; and about this problem there is this also to be said. **47** Of existing things some, they say, are sensible, others intelligible, and the latter are apprehended by the reason, the former by the senses, and the senses are "simply-passive,"* while the reason proceeds from the apprehension of sensibles to the apprehension of intelligibles. If then any body exists, it is either sensible or intelligible. Now it is not sensible; for it is supposed to be apprehended as a conglomeration of length and depth and breadth and solidity and color and various other things, along with which it is experienced; whereas, according to their statements, the senses are "simply-passive." And if body is said to be intelligible, **48** there must certainly be preexistent in the nature of things some sensible object from which to derive the notion of bodies, they being intelligible. But nothing

---

*This means that each sense is specialized, so that it is capable of receiving only one kind of impression (e.g., the sight is affected by color, but not by sound or solidity).

exists save body and the incorporeal, and of these the incorporeal is essentially intelligible, and body, as we have shown, is not sensible. Since, then, no sensible object exists in the nature of things from which we can derive the notion of body, body will not be intelligible either. And if it is neither sensible nor intelligible, and besides these nothing else exists, we must declare that, so far as this argument goes, body has **49** no existence. Accordingly we, by thus opposing the arguments against body to the apparent existence of body, infer suspension of judgment concerning body.

The inapprehensibility of body involves also that of the incorporeal. For privations are conceived as privations of states or faculties, as, for example, blindness of sight, deafness of hearing, and similarly with the rest. Hence, in order to apprehend a privation, we must first have apprehended the state of which the privation is said to be a privation; for if one had no conception of sight one would not be able to assert that this man does not possess sight, which is the **50** meaning of being blind. If then incorporeality is the privation of body, and when states are not apprehensible it is impossible for the privations of them to be apprehended, and it has been proved that body is inapprehensible, incorporeality also will be inapprehensible. Moreover, it is either sensible or intelligible. And if it is sensible, it is inapprehensible because of the variance amongst animals and men, the senses and the circumstances, and owing to the admixtures and all the other things we have previously described in our exposition of the ten tropes. If, again, it is intelligible, since the apprehension of sensibles, which is supposed to form the starting point from which we attain the intelligibles, is not immediately given, neither will the apprehension of the intelligibles be given immediately, nor, consequently, that of incorporeality.

Also, he who asserts that he apprehends the **51** incorporeal will maintain that he apprehends it either by sense or by means of reason. Certainly not by sense, since it is supposed that the senses perceive the sensibles by way of "impression" and "indentation,"—take sight, for instance, whether it occur by reason of the tension of a cone,* or of the emissions and immissions of images, or by effusions of rays or colors; and hearing too, whether it be the smitten air or the parts of the sound that are carried round the ears and smite the acoustic breath so as to effect the perception of sound. Smells also impinge on the nose and flavors on the tongue, and likewise objects of touch on the sense of touch. But incorporeals are **52** incapable of submitting to impression of this kind, so that they could not be apprehended by sense.

Nor yet by means of reason. For if the reason is "verbally expressible" and incorporeal, as the Stoics assert, he who says that incorporeals are apprehended by means of reason is begging the question. For when our question is—"Can an incorporeal object be apprehended?" he assumes an incorporeal object and then, by means of it alone, claims to effect the apprehension of incorporeals. Yet reason itself, if it is in-

---

*[I.e., a cone of light connecting eye with object, a theory of vision formulated by Chrysippus.]

corporeal, belongs to the class of things which are
53 in question. How, then, is one to prove that this particular incorporeal (I mean reason) is previously
apprehended? For if it is by means of another incorporeal, we shall ask for the proof of its apprehension also, and so on *ad infinitum;* whereas, if it
is by means of a body, the apprehension of bodies
is also in question; by what means, then, are we to
prove that the body which is assumed in order to
prove the apprehension of the incorporeal reason is
itself being apprehended? If by means of a body, we
are plunged into infinite regress; while if we do so
by means of an incorporeal, we are wrecked on circular
reasoning. Reason, then, since it is incorporeal, remaining thus inapprehensible, no one will be able to say
that by means of it the incorporeal is apprehended.
54   But if reason is a body, inasmuch as about bodies
also there is much controversy as to whether or not
they are apprehended, owing to what is called their
"continual flux,"* which gives rise to the view that
they do not admit of the title "this" and are nonexistent—just as Plato speaks of bodies as "becoming
but never being,"—I am perplexed as to how this
controversy about body is to be settled, as I see that
it cannot be settled, because of the difficulties stated
a moment ago, either by a body or by an incorporeal.
Neither, then, is it possible to apprehend the incor-
55 poreals by reason. And if they are neither objects

---

*[Heracleitus.]

of sense nor apprehended by means of reason, they will not be apprehended at all.

If, then, it is impossible to be positive either about the existence of body or about the incorporeals, we must also suspend judgment concerning the elements, and possibly about the things which lie behind the elements as well, seeing that of these some are bodies, others incorporeals, and both of these are matters of doubt. In fact, when both the active and the material principles, for these reasons, call for suspense of judgment, the doctrine of principles is open to doubt.

CHAPTER VIII. CONCERNING MIXTURE

But, to pass over these problems, how do they explain **56** the production of the compounds from the primary elements, when neither contact and touch nor mixture and blending has any existence at all? For that touch is nothing I showed a moment ago, when I was discussing the subsistence of body; and that the method of mixture is equally impossible on their own showing, I shall briefly demonstrate. For there is much argument about mixture, and the rival views held by the dogmatists* on the problem propounded are well-nigh endless; and hence we might straightway infer, along with the indeterminable controversy, the inapprehensibility of the problem. And we shall for the moment, owing to the design of our treatise, excuse ourselves from answering all their views in

*Especially Aristotle and the Stoics.

detail, deeming that the following remarks will amply suffice for the present.

57   They declare that mixed things are composed of substance and qualities. If so, one must declare either that their substances are blended but not their qualities, or their qualities blended but not their substances any longer, or neither blended with the other, or both unified with each other. But if neither the qualities nor the substances are blended with one another, mixture will be inconceivable; for how will a single sensation result from the things mixed if the things mixed are blended with one another in none of the

58 ways stated above? And if it should be said that the qualities are simply juxtaposed and the substances blended, even so the statement would be absurd; for we do not perceive the qualities in the mixtures as separate objects but as a single sense impression produced by the mixed things. And anyone who should assert that the qualities are blended, but the substances not, would be asserting the impossible; for the reality of the qualities resides in the substances, so that it would be ridiculous to assert that the qualities by themselves, in separation from the substances, are somehow blended with one another, while the substances are left apart void of quality.

59   It only remains to say that both the qualities and the substances of mixed things permeate one another and by their blending produce mixture. But this is a more absurd view than any of the foregoing; for such a mixture is impossible. Thus, for example, if a cup of hemlock juice were blended with ten cups

of water, it will be said that the hemlock is mixed in with all the water; for certainly if one were to take even the least portion of the mixture he would find it full of the potency of the hemlock. Yet if **60** the hemlock is blended in with every particle of the water and is distributed as a whole over the whole volume of the water and through the mutual inter-penetration of both their substances and their quali-ties, so that mixture may in this way result; and if the things so distributed over each other in every particle occupy an equal space, so that they are equal to each other,—then the cup of hemlock will be equal to the ten cups of water, so that the blend must consist of twenty cups or of only two, according to the assumption now made as to the mode of the mixture. And if, again, a cup of water were poured into the twenty cups, then—according to the theory assumed—the quantity is bound to be forty cups or, again, only two, since it is admissible to conceive either the one cup as all the twenty over which it is distributed, or the twenty cups as the one with which they are being equalized. And by thus pouring **61** in a cup at a time and pursuing the same argument it is possible to infer that the twenty cups seen in the blend must be twenty thousand and more, ac-cording to the theory of the mixture assumed, and at the same time only two—a conclusion which reaches the very height of incongruity. Wherefore this theory of mixture also is absurd.

But if mixture cannot come about by the mutual **62** blending either of the substances alone or of the qualities alone or of both or of neither, and it is impossible to conceive any other ways than these, then the process of mixture and of blending in general is inconceivable. Hence, if the so-called elements are unable to form the compounds either by way of contact through juxtapostion or by mixture or blending, then, so far as this argument goes, the physical theory of the dogmatists is inconceivable.

CHAPTER IX. CONCERNING MOTION

63 In addition to the foregoing we might have dwelt on the argument about the kinds of motion, since this also might be held to render the physical theory of the dogmatists impossible. For the formation of the compounds must certainly be due to some motion both of the elements and of the efficient principle. If, then, we shall show that no one kind of motion is generally agreed upon, it will be clear that, even if all the assumptions mentioned above be granted, the dogmatists have elaborated their so-called "physical doctrine" in vain.

CHAPTER X. CONCERNING TRANSIENT MOTION

64 Now those who are reputed to have given the most complete classification of motion assert that six kinds of it exist—local transition, physical change, increase, decrease, becoming, perishing. We, then, shall deal with each of the aforesaid kinds separately beginning with local transition. According, then, to the dogmatists, this is the motion by which the moving object passes on from place to place, either wholly or partially—wholly as in the case of men walking, partially as when a globe is moving around a central axis, for while as a whole it remains in the same place, its parts change their places.

The main views held about motion are, I imagine, **65** three. It is assumed by ordinary people and by some philosophers that motion exists, but by Parmenides, Melissus,* and certain others that it does not exist; while the skeptics have declared that it is "no more" existent than nonexistent; for so far as the evidence of phenomena goes it seems that motion exists, whereas to judge by the philosophic argument it would seem not to exist. So when we have exposed the contradiction which lies between those who believe in the existence of motion and those who maintain that motion is naught, if we shall find the counter-arguments of equal weight, we shall be compelled to declare that, so far as these arguments go, motion is "no more" existent than nonexistent. We shall begin **66** with those who affirm its real existence.

These base their view mainly on "evidence." If, say they, motion does not exist, how does the sun move from east to west, and how does it produce the seasons of the year, which are brought about by its approximations to us and its recessions from

---

*[Parmenides (fl. ca. 450 B.C.) and Melissus (fl. ca. 450 B.C.) were both philosophers of the Eleatic school. Parmenides held that true Being is endless, single, motionless, continuous, and determinate, like a sphere. Melissus differed from Parmenides in maintaining the spatial infinity of the universe.]

us? Or how do ships put out from harbors and cast anchor in other harbors very far distant from the first? And in what fashion does the denier of motion proceed from his house and return to it again? These facts are perfectly incontestable. Consequently, when one of the Cynics had an argument about motion put to him, he made no reply but stood up and began to walk, thus demonstrating by his action and by "evidence" that motion is capable of real existence.

67   So these men attempt in this way to put to shame those who hold the contrary opinion; but those who deny the existence of motion allege such arguments as these: If a thing is moved, it is moved either by itself or by another thing. But if it is moved by another, it will be moved either causelessly or owing to some cause. Nothing, they assert, is moved causelessly; but if it is moved owing to some cause, the cause owing to which it moves will be what makes it move, and thus we are involved in an infinite regress, according to the criticism stated a little while ago. Moreover,

68   if the movent thing is active, and what is active is moved, that movent thing will need another movent thing, and the second a third, and so on *ad infinitum,* so that the motion comes to have no beginning; which is absurd. Therefore the thing that moves is not always moved by another. Nor yet by itself. Since every movent causes motion either by pushing forward or by drawing after or by pushing up or by thrusting down, what is self-movent must move itself in one

69   of the aforesaid ways. But if it moves itself propulsively, it will be behind itself; and if by pulling after, it will be in front of itself; and if by pushing up, it will be below itself; and if by thrusting down, it will be above itself. But it is impossible for anything to be above or before or beneath or behind its own self; therefore it is impossible for anything to be moved by itself. But if nothing is moved either by itself or by another, then nothing is moved at all.

And if anyone should seek refuge in the notions **70** of "impulse" and "purpose" we must remind him of the controversy about "what is in our power," and how it is still unsettled, since hitherto we have failed to find a criterion of truth.

Further, there is also this to be said. If a thing **71** moves, it moves either in the place where it is or in that where it is not. But it does not move in the place where it is, for if it is in it, it remains in it; nor yet does it move in the place where it is not; for where a thing is not, there it can neither effect nor suffer anything. Therefore nothing moves. This argument is, in fact, that of Diodorus Cronos, but it has been the subject of many attacks, of which we shall describe, owing to the character of our treatise, only the more formidable, together with a judgment of their value, as it seems to us.

Some, then, assert that a thing can move in the **72** place where it is; at any rate the globes which revolve around their axes move while remaining in the same place. Against these men we should transfer the argument which applies to each of the parts of the globe, and, reminding them that, to judge by this argument, it does not move even in respect of its

parts, draw the conclusion that nothing moves in
73 the place where it is. And we shall take the same
course in replying to those who declare that the
moving thing occupies two places, that wherein it
is and that whereto it shifts. For we shall ask them
when the moving object shifts from the place wherein
it is to the other place—whether while it is in the
first place or while it is in the second. But when
it is in the first place it does not pass over into the
second, for it is still in the first; and when it is not
74 in this, it is not passing from it. And besides, the
question is being begged; for where it is not, there
it cannot be active. For surely no one will allow that
any object to which he does not grant motion at
all can shift to any place.

75 Some, however, make this statement: Place is
used in two senses, the broad senses, as for example
"my house," and the exact sense, as for instance "the
air which enfolds the surface of my body." So the
moving object is said to move in place, "place" being
used not in the exact sense but in the broad sense.
To these we can reply by dividing up "place" in the
broad sense, and saying that in one part of it the
body said to be moved properly exists, this being
its own "place" in the exact sense, and in the other
part it does not exist, this being the remaining portions
of "place" in the extended sense; next we shall argue
that an object can move neither in the place where
it is nor in that where it is not, and so conclude
that nothing can move even in what is perversely
termed "place" in the broad sense; for this is composed

of the place wherein it is in the exact sense and the place wherein it is not, and it has been proved that a thing cannot move in either of these.

We should also propound the following argument. If a thing moves it moves either by way of orderly, or gradual, progression or by occupying the divisible interval all at once; but in neither of these ways can a thing move, as we shall prove; so that it does not move at all. **76**

Now that a thing cannot move in orderly progression is plain on the face of it. For if bodies, and also the places and the times in which the bodies are said to move, are divided into infinity, motion will not occur, it being impossible to discover amongst the infinite any first thing wherefrom the object said to move will derive its initial movement. And if the aforesaid objects are reducible to atomic parts, and each of the moving things passes equally in an atomic period of time with its own first atom into the first atomic point of space, then all moving things are of equal velocity—the speediest horse, for instance, and the tortoise; which is a result even more absurd than the former. Therefore motion does not take place by way of orderly progression. **77**

Nor yet by way of immediate occupation of the divisible interval. For if one ought, as they declare, to take the apparent as evidence for the nonapparent, since, in order to complete the distance of a stade a man must first complete the first portion of the stade, and secondly the second portion, and so on with the rest, so likewise everything that moves ought to move **78** by way of orderly progression; for surely if we should assert that the moving thing passes all at once through all the portions of the place wherein it is said to move, it will be in all the portion thereof at once, and if one portion of the place through which it has its motion should be cold, another hot, or, mayhap, one black, another white, so as to be able also to color things in contact,—then the moving thing will be at once hot and cold and black and white, which is absurd.

79 Next let them tell us how much space the moving thing passes through all at once. For if they shall assert that it is limitless, they will be granting that a thing moves through the whole of the earth all at once; while if they shirk this conclusion, let them define for us the extent of the space. But, on the one hand, the attempt to define precisely the space or interval beyond which the thing moving all at once will be unable to advance so much as a hair's breadth is probably not merely presumptuous and rash or even ridiculous, but plunges us again into the original difficulty; for all things will be of equal velocity, if each of them alike has its transitional movements over definite inter-

80 vals of space. And if, on the other hand, they shall assert that the moving thing moves all at once through a space that is small but not precisely determined, it will be open to us to adopt the *sorites* argument and keep constantly adding a hair's breadth of space to the breadth assumed. And if, then, they shall make a halt anywhere while we are pursuing this argument, they will be reverting to the monstrous theory of precise definition as before; while if they shall assent to the

process of addition, we shall force them to grant that a thing can move all at once through the whole of the earth. Consequently, objects said to be in motion do not move by occupying a divisible interval all at once. But if a thing moves neither thus instantaneously **81** nor by way or gradual progression, it does not move at all.

These, and yet more than these, are the arguments used by those who reject transient motion. But we, being unable to refute either these arguments or the apparent facts upon which the view of reality of motion is based, suspend our judgment—in view of the contradiction between appearances and arguments—regarding the question as to the existence or nonexistence of motion.

CHAPTER XI. CONCERNING INCREASE AND DECREASE

Employing the same reasoning we suspend judgment **82** also concerning both increase and decrease. For the outward evidence seems to support their reality, which the arguments seem to refute. For just consider: That which increases must grow in size as a stable substance, so that it will be false for anyone to say that one thing increases when an addition is made to another. Since then substance* is never stable but always in flux, one part supplanting another, the thing said to have increased does not retain its former substance together with the added substance but has

---

*I.e., material substance, which Heracleitus and Plato said was "in flux."

83 its substance all different. Just as if, for example, when there is a beam three cubits long a man should bring another of ten cubits and declare that the beam of three cubits had increased, he would be lying because the one is wholly different from the other; so too in the case of every object which is said to increase, as the former matter flows away and fresh matter enters in its place, if what is said to be added is added, one should not call such a condition increase but complete alteration.

84 The same argument applies also to decrease. For how could that which has no stable existence be said to have decreased? Besides, if decrease takes place by way of subtraction, and increase by addition, and neither subtraction nor addition is anything, then neither decrease nor increase is anything.

CHAPTER XII. CONCERNING SUBTRACTION AND ADDITION

85 That subtraction is nothing they argue thus: If anything is subtracted from anything, either equal is subtracted from equal, or greater from less, or less from greater. But in none of these ways does subtraction take place, as we shall show; therefore subtraction is impossible.

That subtraction takes place in none of these ways is plain from what follows: What is subtracted from anything ought, before its subtraction, to be **86** included in that from which it is subtracted. But the equal is not included in the equal—six, for instance, in six; for what includes must be greater than what is included, and that from which the subtraction is made than what is subtracted, in order that there may be some remainder after the subtraction; for it is this which is held to distinguish subtraction from complete removal. Nor is the greater included in the less—six, for instance, in five; for that is irrational. And for this reason, neither is the less included in **87** the greater. For if five is included in six, as less in greater, four will be included in five, three in four, two in three, and one in two. Therefore six will contain five, four, three, two, and one, which when put together form the number fifteen, and this we conclude is included in six, if it be granted that the less is included in the greater. So likewise in the fifteen which is included in the six there is included the number thirty-five,* and so on, step by step, to infinity. But it is absurd to say that infinite numbers are included in the number six; and so it is also absurd to say that less is included in greater. If, then, what is **88** subtracted from a thing must be included in that from which it is to be subtracted, and neither equal is included in equal, nor greater in less, nor less in greater, then nothing is subtracted from anything.

Again, if anything is subtracted from anything, it is either a whole subtracted from a whole, or a part from a part, or a whole from a part, or a part from a whole. But to say that a whole is subtracted **89**

---

*The addition of the numbers 1 . . . 5 gives 15; of 1 . . . 4, 10; of 1 . . . 3, 6; of 1 and 2, 3; so we get the total 35 = 15 + 10 + 6 + 3 + 1.

from either a whole or a part is plainly nonsense. It remains, then, to say that a part is subtracted either from a whole or from a part; which is absurd. Thus for example—basing our argument on numbers for the sake of clearness—let us take ten and suppose that from it one is subtracted. This one, then, cannot be subtracted either from the whole ten or from the remaining part of the ten, as I shall show; therefore it is not subtracted at all.

90   For if the one is subtracted from the whole ten, since the ten is neither something other than the ten ones nor one of the ones, but the aggregate of the ones, the one ought to be subtracted from each of the ones in order to be subtracted from the whole ten. Now from a one, above all, nothing can be subtracted; for the ones are indivisible, and on this account the one will not be subtracted from the ten 91 in this way. And even were we to grant that the one is subtracted from each of the ones, the one will contain ten parts, and as containing ten parts it will be a ten. And further, since ten other parts remain, after the subtraction of the ten parts of the so-called one, the ten will be twenty. But it is absurd to say that the one is ten and the ten twenty, and to divide what, according to them,* is indivisible. Wherefore it is absurd to say that the one is subtracted from the whole ten.

92   Neither is the one subtracted from the remaining nine; for that from which anything is subtracted does

---

*I.e., the dogmatists, who assumed the indivisibility of the "one."

not remain entire, but the nine does remain entire after the subtraction of that one. Besides, since the nine is nothing more than the nine ones, if it should be said that the one is subtracted from the whole nine, the sum subtracted will be nine, or if from a part of it, then in case it be eight the same absurd results will follow, while if the subtraction is made from the last one, they will be affirming the divisibility of that one, which is absurd. So then, neither from **93** the nine is the one subtracted. But if it is neither subtracted from the whole ten nor from a part of it, no part can be subtracted from either a whole or a part. If, then, nothing is subtracted either as whole from whole or as part from whole, nor as whole from part or as part from part, then nothing is subtracted from anything.

Moreover, addition is regarded by them* as one **94** of the impossibles. For, they say, that which is added is added either to itself or to what preexists or to the compound of both; but none of these alternatives is sound; therefore nothing is added to anything. Suppose, for instance, a measure of four cups, and add to this a cup. To what, I ask, is it added? For it cannot be added to itself, since what is added must be other than that whereto it is added, but nothing is other than itself. Neither is it added to the com- **95** pound of the four cups and the one cup; for how could anything be added to what does not yet exist? Besides, if the added cup is blended with the four

*The skeptics.

cups and the one cup, six cups will be the measure resulting from the four cups and the one cup and

96 the added cup. And if the cup is added to the four cups alone, since that which is extended over anything is equal to that which it extends, the cup which extends over the measure of four cups will double the four cups so that the whole measure becomes eight cups— a result contrary to experience. If, then, what is said to be added is neither added to itself nor to what preexists nor to the compound of these, and besides these there are no other alternatives, then there is no addition of anything to anything.

CHAPTER XIII. CONCERNING TRANSPOSITION

97 Together with the existence of addition and subtraction and local motion transposition also is abolished, for this is subtraction from a thing and addition to a thing by way of transition.

CHAPTER XIV. CONCERNING WHOLE AND PART

98 So too with whole and part. For the whole is held to come about by the combination and addition of the parts, and to cease from being a whole by the subtraction of one or more parts. Besides, if a whole exists, it is either other than its parts* or its parts

99 themselves form the whole. Now it is apparent that the whole is nothing other than its parts; for certainly

---

*The view of Epicurus; the Stoics said that the whole is neither the same as its parts nor different.

when the parts are removed there is nothing left, so as to enable us to account the whole as something else besides its parts. But if the parts themselves form the whole, the whole will be merely a name and an empty title, and it will have no individual existence, just as separation also is nothing apart from the things separated, or laying beams apart from the beams laid. Therefore no whole exists.

Nor yet parts. For if parts exist, either they are **100** parts of the whole, or of one another, or each one of itself. But they are not parts of the whole, since it is nothing else than its parts (and besides, the parts will on this assumption be parts of themselves, since each of the parts is said to be complementary to the whole); nor yet of one another, since the part is said to be included in that whereof it is part, and it is absurd to assert that, say, the hand is included in the foot. Neither will each be a part of itself; for, **101** because of the inclusion, it will be both greater and less than itself. If, then, the so-called parts are parts neither of the whole nor of themselves nor of one another, they are parts of nothing. But if they are parts of nothing, parts have no existence; for co-relatives are annulled together.

Let thus much be said, then, of a general character, by way of digression, seeing that once already we have dealt with the subject of whole and part.

CHAPTER XV. CONCERNING PHYSICAL CHANGE

102 Some, too, maintain that what is called "physical change" is nonreal, and the arguments they employ are such as these: If a thing changes, what changes is either corporeal or incorporeal; but each of these **103** is a matter of dispute; therefore the theory of change will also be disputable. If a thing changes, it changes through certain actions of a Cause and by being acted upon. But it does not change by being acted upon, for the neality of Cause is refuted, and therewith is refuted also the object which is acted upon, as it has **104** no agent to act upon it. Therefore nothing changes at all. If a thing changes, either what is changes or what is not. Now what is not is unreal and can neither act nor be acted upon at all, so that it does not admit of change either. And if what is changes, it changes either in so far as it is in being or in so far as it **105** is not in being. Now in so far as it is not in being it does not change, for it is not even existent; while if it changes in so far as it is existent, it will be other than existent, which means that it will be nonexistent. But it is absurd to say that the existent becomes nonexistent; therefore the existent does not change either. And if neither the existent nor the nonexistent changes, and besides these there is nothing else, it only remains to say that nothing changes.

106 Some also argue thus: That which changes must change in a certain time; but nothing changes either in the past or in the future, nor yet in the present, as we shall prove; nothing therefore changes. Nothing changes in the past or in the future, for neither of these times is present, and it is impossible to do or suffer anything in time that is not existent and present. Nor yet in time present. For the present time is **107** probably also unreal, and—even if we set aside this point—it is indivisible; and it is impossible to suppose that in an indivisible moment of time iron, say, changes from hard to soft, or any one of all the other changes takes place; for they appear to require extension in time. If, then, nothing changes either in the past or in the future or in the present, we must declare that nothing changes at all.

Further, if change exists at all it is either sensible **108** or intelligible; but it is not sensible, since the senses are specialized, whereas change is thought to possess "concurrent recollection" both of that from which it changes and that into which it is said to change. And if it is intelligible, then, since (as we have frequently pointed out already) there exists among the ancients an unsettled controversy as to the reality of intelligibles, we shall also be unable to make any assertion about the reality of change.

CHAPTER XVI. CONCERNING BECOMING AND PERISHING

Both becoming and perishing are included in the **109** refutation of addition and subtraction and physical change; for apart from these nothing would become or perish. Thus, for instance, it is as a result of the perishing of the ten, as they say, that the nine becomes by the subtraction of one, and the ten from the perishing of the nine by the addition of one; and rust becomes from the perishing of bronze by means of change. Hence, if the aforesaid motions are abolished it is likely that becoming and perishing are also necessarily abolished.

110   Yet none the less some argue also as follows: If Socrates was born, Socrates became either when Socrates existed not or when Socrates already existed; but if he shall be said to have become when he already existed, he will have become twice; and if when he did not exist, Socrates was both existent and nonexistent at the same time—existent through having become, **111** nonexistent by hypothesis. And if Socrates died, he died either when he lived or when he died. Now he did not die when he lived, since he would have been at once both alive and dead; nor yet when he died, since he would have been dead twice. Therefore Socrates did not die. And by applying this argument in turn to each of the things said to become or perish it is possible to abolish becoming and perishing.

112   Some also argue thus: If a thing becomes, either the existent becomes or the nonexistent. But the nonexistent does not become; for to the nonexistent nothing can occur; neither, therefore, can becoming occur. Nor does the existent become. For if the existent becomes, it becomes either in so far as it is existent or in so far as it is nonexistent. Now in so far as it is nonexistent it does not become. But if it becomes in so far as it is existent, then, since they assert that what becomes becomes other from other,* what becomes will be other than the existent, and that is nonexistent. Therefore what becomes will be nonexistent, which is nonsense. If, then, neither **113** the nonexistent becomes nor the existent, nothing becomes at all.

For the same reasons, neither does anything perish. For if anything perishes, it is either the existent that perishes or the nonexistent. Now the nonexistent does not perish, for what perishes must be the subject of action. Nor yet does the existent perish. For it must perish either while continuing in existence or while not so continuing. And if it be while continuing in existence, it will be at one and the same time both existent and nonexistent; for since it does not perish **114** in so far as it is nonexistent but in so far as it is existent, it will be other than the existent and therefore nonexistent in so far as it is said to have perished, whereas in so far as it is said to perish while continuing in existence it will be existent. But it is absurd to say that the same thing is both existent and nonexistent; therefore the existent does not perish while continuing in existence. And if the existent does not perish while continuing in existence but passes first into nonexistence and then in this way perishes, it is no longer the existent that perishes but the nonexistent; and this we have shown to be impossible. If, then, neither the existent perishes nor the nonexistent, and besides these there is nothing else, nothing perishes at all.

---

*I.e., it is ("other" or) different after it has "become" from what it was before it "became": "becoming" involves a change of nature or character in the thing which undergoes the process.

This account of the motions will suffice by way of outline, and therefrom it follows that the physical science of the dogmatists is unreal and inconceivable.

CHAPTER XVII. CONCERNING REST

115 In like manner some have doubted about physical rest, saying that what is in motion is not at rest, but every body is constantly in motion according to the views of the dogmatists who assert that being is in flux and always undergoing effluxes and additions—just as Plato does not even speak of bodies as "being" but rather calls them "becoming," and Heracleitus compares the mobility of our matter*

116 to the swift current of a river. Therefore no body is at rest. What is said to be at rest is, in fact, held to be embraced by the things which surround it, and what is embraced is acted upon; but nothing acted upon exists, since no causal activity exists, as we have shown; therefore nothing is at rest.

Some, too, propound this argument: What is at rest is acted upon; but what is acted upon is in motion; therefore what is said to be at rest is in motion; but

117 if it is in motion, it is not at rest. And from this it is evident that neither does the incorporeal admit of being at rest. For if what is at rest is acted upon, and being acted upon is a property, if anything, of bodies and not of incorporeals, no incorporeal can either be acted upon or be at rest; therefore nothing is at rest.

---

*"Matter" in the ordinary sense of "our" physical universe, as distinct from any logical or metaphysical use of the term.

So much for the subject of rest. And since no **118** one of the things we have mentioned is conceived apart from space or time, we must pass on to consider these; for if one should prove these to be unreal, then, because of them, each of the others also will be unreal. Let us begin with space.

CHAPTER XVIII. CONCERNING SPACE

Space, or place, then, is used in two senses, the strict **119** and the loose—loosely of place taken broadly (as "my city"), and strictly of exactly containing place whereby we are exactly enclosed. Our inquiry, then, is concerned with space of the strict kind. This some* have affirmed, others denied; and others have suspended judgment about it. And of these, those **120** who maintain its existence have recourse to the evidence of experience. Who, they argue, could assert that space does not exist when he sees the parts of space, such as right and left, up and down, before and behind; and when he is now here, now there, and sees that where my teacher† was talking there I am talking now; and when he observes that the place of things naturally light is different from that of things naturally heavy; and when, also, he hears **121** the ancients declaring that "Verily first of all came Chaos into existence"‡? For space, they say, is called

---

*E.g., The Stoics and Peripatetics.

†Herodotus of Tarsus, [who belonged to the pneumatic school of medicine. The pneumatic school accepted the predominance of *pneuma*, i.e., breath, as the vital principle].

‡Hesiod, *Theogony,* 118.

Chaos from its capacity for containing* what becomes within it. Then, too, if any body exists, space also exists; for without it body would not exist. And if "that *by* which" exists, and "that *from* which," there exists also "that *in* which," and this is space; but the first is in each of the two, therefore the second is in both.

122   But those who deny space do not admit the existence of the parts of space; for space, they say, is nothing else than its parts, and he who tries to deduce the existence of space from the assumption that its parts exist is seeking to establish the matter in question by means of itself. Equally silly is the language of those who assert that a thing becomes or has become in some place, when space in general is not admitted. And they also presume the reality of body, which is not self-evident; and, in much the same way as space, both "that *from* which" and "that *by* which"

123   are proved to be unreal. Hesiod, too, is no competent judge of philosophical problems. And while thus rebutting the arguments that tend to establish the existence of space, they also demonstrate its unreality more elaborately by making use of what are held to be the most weighty views of the dogmatists about space, namely those of the Stoics and Peripatetics, in the following fashion.

124   The Stoics declare that void is that which is capable of being occupied by an existent but is not

---

*"Chaos" is here absurdly derived from *chora*, "room" (the Stoics connected it with *chein*, "to pour"). It means, in fact, a "cavity" or abyss (from *chaskein*, "to yawn").

so occupied, or an interval empty of body, or an interval unoccupied by body; and that place is an interval occupied by an existent and equated to that which occupies it ("existent" being here the name they give to "body"); and that room is an interval partly occupied by body and partly unoccupied—though some of them say that room is the place of the large body, so that the difference between place and room depends on size. Their opponents then argue thus: **125** When the Stoics define place as an "interval occupied by body," in what sense do they call it an "interval"? Do they mean the length of the body or its width or its depth only, or all three dimensions? For if they mean one dimension, the place is not equated with the object of which it is the place, and besides, that which includes is part of what is included, which is pure nonsense. And if by "interval" is meant the **126** three dimensions, then, since in the so-called place there subsists neither a void nor another body which has dimensions, but only the body said to exist in place, and it is composed of the dimensions (for it is length and breadth and depth and solidity, this last being said to be a property of the foregoing dimensions), the body itself will be its own place and at once both container and contained, which is absurd. Therefore no dimension of a subsisting place exists. **127** And, consequently, place is nothing.

This argument also is propounded. Since the dimensions are not found to be twofold in the case of each of the objects said to exist in place, but there is one length, one breadth, and one depth, do these dimensions belong to the body only, or to the place only, or to both? If they belong only to the place, the body will have no length or breadth or depth of its own, so that the body will not even be the

128 body, which is absurd. If they belong to both, then, since the void had no reality apart from the dimensions, if the dimensions of the void subsist in the body and serve to compose the body itself, the components of the void will also be components of the body—for about the reality of solidity it is impossible to say anything positive, as we have shown above. And since in the case of the so-called body only those dimensions appear which belong to the void and are identical with the void, the body will be void, which is absurd. And if the dimensions belong to the body only, there will be no dimension of place, and therefore no place either. If, then, no dimension of place is found in any of the ways described above, place does not exist.

129   Further, it is argued that when the body occupies the void and place comes about, the void either remains or withdraws or perishes. But if it remains, the plenum and the void will be identical; and if it withdraws by a movement of transition, or perishes by change, the void will be a body; for these affections are peculiar to body. But it is absurd to say either that void and plenum are identical or that the void is body. Therefore it is absurd to say that the void can be occupied by body and become place. For

130 these reasons also the void is found to be unreal, since it is impossible for it to be occupied by body and to become place; for void was defined as "that which is capable of being occupied by body." And, in the refutation of these, room also is involved; for it is annulled along with place if "room is the large place," while if it is "that which is partly occupied by body and partly empty extension," its refutation is included in that of these two.

These arguments, and others besides, are directed against the views about place held by the Stoics. The Peripatetics assert that place is "the limit of what **131** encloses in so far as it encloses," so that my place is the surface of the air that forms a mold round my body. But if this is place, the same thing will both be and not be. For when the body is about to become in a certain place, then, inasmuch as nothing can become in what is nonexistent, the place must be preexistent in order that the body may in this way become in it, and consequently the place will exist before the-body-in-the-place becomes therein. But inasmuch as it consists in the molding of the surface of what encloses round the thing enclosed, place cannot be already subsisting before the body becomes within it, and therefore it will not be in existence then. But it absurd to say that the same thing both is and is not; therefore place is not "the limit of what encloses in so far as it encloses."

Furthermore, if place is anything, it is either **132** created or uncreate. Now it is not uncreate; for it is brought about, they say, by being molded round the body within it. Nor yet is it created; for if it is created, it is either when the body is in place that the place, in which the body in place is already said to be, comes into existence, or when the body is **133** not in it. But it does not come into existence either when the body is in it (for the place of the body within in exists already), or when it is not in it, since, as they assert, the container is molded round the contained and in this way place becomes, and nothing can be molded round that which is not within it. But if place does not become either when the body is in place or when it is not therein, and no other alternatives are conceivable, then place is not created at all. And if it is neither created nor uncreate, it has no existence.

134 These objections may also be stated more generally. If place is anything, it is either corporeal or incorporeal; but each of these alternatives is, as we have shown, disputed; therefore place is in dispute. Place is conceived in relation to the body whereof it is the place; but the doctrine of the reality of body is disputed, therefore that of place is likewise disputable. The place of each thing is not eternal, but if we say that it becomes it is found to be unreal as becoming does not exist.

135 It is possible to adduce many other arguments. But in order to avoid prolonging our exposition, we may conclude by saying that while the skeptics are put to confusion by the arguments, they are also put to shame by the evidence of experience. Consequently we attach ourselves to neither side, so far as concerns the doctrines of the dogmatists, but suspend judgment regarding place.

CHAPTER XIX. CONCERNING TIME

Our attitude is the same with respect to the inquiry **136** about time. For if we depend on appearances, time seems to be something, but if we depend on the arguments about it, it appears unreal. Some* define time as "the interval of the motion of the whole" (meaning by "whole" the universe), others as "the actual motion of the universe"; Aristotle (or, as some say, Plato) as "the number of the prior and posterior in motion"; Strato (or, as some say, Aristotle) as **137** "the measure of motion and rest"; Epicurus (according to Demetrius the Laconian†) as "a concurrence of concurrences, concomitant with days and nights and seasons and affections and nonaffections and motions and rests." And, in point of substance, some **138** have affirmed that it is corporeal—for instance, Aenesidemus, arguing that it differs in nothing from being and the prime body,—others,‡ that it is incorporeal. Either, then, all these theories are true, or all false, or some true and some false; but they cannot all be true (most of them being in conflict), nor will it be granted by the dogmatists that all are false. And besides, should it be granted that the assertion **139** of the corporeality of time is false, and that of its incorporeality likewise false, then, *ipso facto,* the unreality of time will be granted; for it cannot be anything but one or other of these. Nor yet can we

---

*The Stoics.
†An Epicurean [second century B.C.].
‡The Stoics.

apprehend which theories are true, which false, owing to the equal weight of the rival opinions as well as the perplexity regarding the criterion and proof.

140 Hence for these reasons we shall be unable to affirm anything positively about time.

Further, since time does not seem to subsist without motion or even rest, if motion is abolished, and likewise rest, time is abolished. None the less the following objections against time are made by some. If time exists, it is either limited or unlimited.

141 But if it is limited, it began at a certain time and will end at a certain time. Consequently, there was once a time when time was not (before it began), and there will once be a time when time will not be (after it has ended); which is absurd. So then time

142 is not limited. But if it is unlimited, since part of it is said to be past, part present, and part future, the future and past are either existent or nonexistent. But if they are nonexistent, and there remains only the present, which is momentary, time will be limited and the original difficulties will follow. And if the past exists and the future exists, each of these will be present. But it is absurd to call past and future time present; neither, then, is time unlimited. But if it is neither unlimited nor limited, time does not exist at all.

143 Further, if time exists it is either divisible or indivisible. Now it is not indivisible; for it is divided, as they themselves declare, into present, past, and future. Yet it is not divisible either. For each divisible thing is measured by some part of itself, the measure coinciding with each part of the measured, as when we measure a cubit by a finger. But time cannot be measured by any part of itself. If, for instance, the present measures the past, it will coincide with the past and will therefore be past, and similarly it will be future in the case of the future. And if the future should measure the rest, it will be present and past, and so likewise the past will be future and present; which is nonsense. Neither, then, is time divisible. But if it is neither indivisible nor divisible, it does not exist.

Time, too, is said to be tripartite, partly past, **144** partly present, and partly future. Of these the past and the future are nonexistent; for if past and future time exist now, each of them will be present. Neither is the present existent; for if present time exists it is either indivisible or divisible. Now it is not indivisible; for what changes is said to change in the present time, but nothing changes in indivisible time— iron, for instance, into softness, and so on. Hence present time is not indivisible. Neither is it divisible; **145** for it could not be divided into a plurality of presents, since time present is said to change into time past imperceptibly owing to the rapid flux of the things in the universe. Nor yet into past and future; for so it will be unreal, having one part of itself no longer existent and the other part not yet existent. Hence, too, the present cannot be the end of the past and **146** the beginning of the future, since then it will both be and not be existent; for it will exist as present, but will not exist because its parts are nonexistent.

Therefore it is not divisible either. But if the present is neither indivisible nor divisible, it does not exist. And when neither the present nor the past nor the future exists, time too is nonexistent; for what is compounded of things unreal is unreal.

147 This argument, too, is alleged against time: If time exists it is either generable and perishable or ingenerable and imperishable. Now it is not ingenerable and imperishable, since part of it is said to be past and no longer in existence, and part to be future and not yet in existence. Neither is it generable and perishable. For things generated must **148** be generated from something existent, and things which perish must perish into something existent, according to the postulates of the dogmatists themselves. If, then, time perishes into the past, it perishes into a nonexistent; and if it is generated out of the future, it is generated out of a nonexistent; for neither of these is in existence. But it is absurd to say that anything is generated from a nonexistent or perishes into the nonexistent. Therefore time is not generable and perishable. But if it is neither ingenerable and imperishable nor generable and perishable, it does not exist at all.

149 Further, since everything which becomes seems to become in time, time, if it becomes, becomes in time. Either, then, it becomes itself in itself or as one time in another. But if it becomes in itself, it will be at once both existent and nonexistent. For since that within which a thing becomes must exist before the thing which becomes within it, the time which becomes in itself does not yet exist in so far as it becomes, but does already exist in so far as it becomes in itself. Consequently it does not become **150** in itself. Nor yet in another. For if the present becomes in the future, the present will be future, and if in the past, it will be past. And the same may be said of all the other times; so that one time does not become in another. But if time neither becomes in itself nor as one time in another it is not generable. And it has been shown that it is not ingenerable either. Being, then, neither generable nor ingenerable, it is wholly nonexistent; for each existing thing is bound to be either generable or ingenerable.

Chapter XX. Concerning Number

Since time, it seems, is not found apart from number, **151** it will not be out of place to discuss number briefly. In the customary way we speak undogmatically of numbering a thing and hear number talked of as something which exists; but the extreme methods of the dogmatists have provoked the attack upon number also. Thus, for example, the school of Pythago- **152** ras declare that numbers are also elements of the universe. They assert, in fact, that phenomena are constructed from something, and that the elements must be simple; therefore the elements are nonevident. But of things nonevident, some are corporeal, like atoms and masses, others incorporeal, like figures*

---

*I.e., the limits of bodies.

and forms and numbers. Of these the corporeal are composite, being constructed from length and breadth and depth and solidity, or even weight. The elements, therefore, are not only nonevident but also incor-

153 poreal. Moreover, each of the incorporeals involves the perception of number, for it is either one or two or more. Thus it is inferred that the nonevident and incorporeal numbers which are involved in all perception are the elements of existing things. Yet not simply these numbers, but both the monad also and the indefinite dyad which is generated by the expansion of the monad, and by participation in

154 which the particular dyads become dyads. For they say that it is from these that the rest of the numbers are generated—those, that is, which are involved in the perception of numerables—and the universe is arranged. For the point presents the relation, or character, of the monad,* and the line that of the dyad (it being regarded as lying between two points), and the surface that of the triad (for they describe it as a flowing of the line breadthwise up to another point placed transversely), and the solid body that of the tetrad; for body is formed by an ascension

155 of the surface up to a point placed above. It is in this way that they image forth both the bodies and the whole universe, which they also declare to be arranged according to harmonic ratios†—namely,

---

*I.e., it is an indivisible unit, and begins the line as the one begins the number-series.

†The terms here used are those of the Pythagorean musical ("octave") system, and denote the ratios 4/:/3, 3/:2, 2/:1.

that of the "by fours," which is "epitrite," as is the ratio of 8 to 6; and that of the "by fives," which is one and a half times, as is the ratio of 9 to 6; and that of the "by alls," which is double, as is the ratio of 12 to 6.

These are the fictions they imagine; and they **156** also make out that number is something else apart from numerables, arguing that if "animal" according to its proper definition is (say) one, the plant, since it is not an animal, will not be one; but the plant is one; therefore the animal is not one *qua* animal, but in virtue of some other attribute perceived outside itself, whereof each animal partakes and because of which it becomes one. And if number is the numerables, since the numerables are men (say) and oxen and horses, number will be men and oxen and horses—and number will be white and black and bearded, if the objects counted should happen to be such. But these things are absurd; therefore number **157** is not the numerables, but it has a reality of its own apart from them whereby it is involved in the perception of the numerables and is an element.

So when they had thus concluded that number is not the numerables, there arose in consequence the difficulty about number. For it is argued that if number exists, number is either the actual numerables or something else apart from them; but number is neither the actual numerables, as the Pythagoreans have proved, nor something else apart from them, as we shall show; number, therefore, is nothing.

That number is nothing apart from the numer- **158**

ables we shall demonstrate by basing our argument
on the monad, for the sake of lucidity of exposition.
If the monad, by partaking in which each of its
participants becomes one, is in itself a real object,
this monad will be either one or as many as are
its participants. But if it is one, does each of the
things said to partake thereof partake of all of it
or of a part of it? For if the one man (say) takes
all the monad, there will no longer exist a monad
for the one horse to partake of, or the one dog or
any one of all the other things which we declare
159 to be one—just as, supposing there are a number
of naked men, who possess only one garment amongst
them, which one man had put on, all the rest will
remain naked and without a garment. And if each
thing partakes of a part of it, then, in the first place,
the monad will have a part, and parts, too, infinite
in number into which it is divided; which is absurd.
And further, just as the part of the decad, such as
the dyad, is not a decad, so neither will the part
of the monad be a monad, and for this reason nothing
will partake of the monad. Hence the monad whereof
the particular objects are said to partake is not one.

160   But if the monads, by participation in which
each of the particular objects is called one, are equal
in number to the numerables to which the term "one"
is applied, the monads partaken of will be infinite
in number. And these either partake of a superior
monad or of monads equal in number to themselves,
or else they do not so partake but are monads apart
161 from any participation. Yet if these can be monads

without participation, each of the sensibles also will be able to be one without participation in a monad, and so at once the monad said to be perceived as real in itself is overthrown. Whereas, if those monads are monads by participation, either they all partake of one monad, or each partakes of a monad of its own. And if all partake of one, each will be said to partake either of a part or of the whole, and the original difficulties will still remain; but if each **162** partakes of its own monad, we must posit a new monad for each of these monads, and others again for the former, and so on *ad infinitum*. If then, in order to apprehend that there are certain self-subsistent monads by participation in which each existing thing is one, it is necessary to apprehend an infinite infinity of intelligible monads, and to apprehend an infinite infinity of intelligible monads is a thing impossible, then it is impossible to show that there are certain intelligible monads and that each existing thing is one through becoming one by participation in its own monad.

It is absurd, therefore, to say that the monads **163** are as numerous as the things which partake of them. But if the so-called self-subsistent monad is neither one nor as many as its participants, a self-subsistent monad does not exist at all. So likewise none of the other numbers will be self-subsistent; for one may apply to all the numbers the argument which has now been employed in the typical case of the monad. But if number is neither self-subsistent, as we have shown, nor consists in the actual numerables, as the

Pythagoreans have demonstrated, and beyond these there is no other alternative, then we must declare that number does not exist.

164　In what way, too, is the dyad said to be generated from the monad by those who believe that number is something else apart from the numerables? For when we combine a monad with another monad either something external is added to the monads, or something is subtracted from them, or nothing is either added or subtracted. But if nothing is either added or subtracted, there will not be a dyad. For neither did the monads, when existing apart from each other, contain the dyad as involved in the perception of them, according to their own definition, nor has any addition now been made to them from without, just as, by **165** hypothesis, nothing has been subtracted. Hence the combination of the monad with the monad will not be a dyad, as no addition or subtraction from without takes place. But if subtraction does take place, not only will there not be a dyad but the monads will even be diminished. And if the dyad is added to them from without, so that a dyad may be generated from the monads, the things which appear to be two will be four; for there exists already a monad and a second monad, and when an outside dyad is added to these **166** the result will be the number four. And the same argument applies to all the other numbers which are said to be formed as a result of combination.

If, then, the numbers which are said to be compounded from the superior numbers are formed neither by subtraction nor by addition nor without subtraction and addition, the formation of the number which is said to be independent and apart from the numerables is noncomposite. But they themselves make it clear that the numbers formed by combination are not ungenerated by asserting that they are compounded and generated from the superior numbers—from the monad, for example, and the indefinite dyad. So then number does not subsist of itself. But if number neither is conceived as self-existent, nor subsists in the numerables, then, to judge from the subtleties introduced by the dogmatists, number is nothing. **167**

Let this, then, suffice as an account in outline of what is called the physical section of philosophy.

CHAPTER XXI. CONCERNING THE ETHICAL DIVISION OF PHILOSOPHY

There remains the ethical division, which is supposed to deal with the distinguishing of things good,* bad, and indifferent. In order, then, to treat of this branch also in a summary way, we shall inquire into the reality of things good, bad, and indifferent, explaining first the conception of each. **168**

CHAPTER XXII. CONCERNING THINGS GOOD, BAD, AND INDIFFERENT

The Stoics, then, assert that good is "utility or not other than utility," meaning by "utility" virtue and **169**

---

*Literally "fair": the Stoics used *kalon* [fair, i.e., beautiful] as a synonym for *agathon* ("good"), and in this section the terms are used as synonymous.

right action, and by "not other than utility" the good man and the friend. For "virtue," as consisting in a certain state of the ruling principle, and "right action," being an activity in accordance with virtue, are exactly "utility"; while the good man and the

170 friend are "not other than utility." For utility is a part of the good man, being his ruling principle. But the wholes, they say, are not the same as the parts (for the man is not a hand), nor are they other than the parts (for without the parts they do not subsist). Wherefore they assert that the wholes are not other than the parts. Hence, since the good man stands in the relation of a whole to his ruling principle, which they have identified with utility, they declare that he is not other than utility.

171 Hence also they assert that good has three meanings. In one of its meanings, good, they say, is that by which utility may be gained, this being the most principal good and virtue; in another meaning, good is that of which utility is an accidental result, like virtue and virtuous actions; and thirdly, it is that which is capable of being useful; and such is virtue and virtuous action and the good man and the friend, and gods and good demons; so that the second signification of good is inclusive of the first signification,

172 and the third of both the second and the first. But some define good as "what is to be chosen for its own sake"; and others as "that which contributes to happiness or is supplementary thereto"; and happiness, as the Stoics declare, is "the smooth current of life."

These, or such as these, are their statements with reference to the notion of the good. But in describing **173** as good what is useful or what is choiceworthy for its own sake or what is contributory to happiness, one is not exhibiting the essence of the good but stating one of its properties. And this is senseless. For the properties aforesaid belong either to the good only or to other things as well. But if they belong to other things as well, they are not, when thus extended, characteristic marks of the good; while if they belong only to the good, it is not possible for us to derive from them a notion of the good. For **174** just as the man who has no notion of "horse" has no knowledge of what "neighing" is and cannot arrive thereby at a notion of "horse," unless he should first meet with a neighing horse, so too one who is seeking the essence of the good, because he has no knowledge of the good, cannot perceive the attribute which is peculiar to it alone in order that he may be enabled thereby to gain a notion of the good itself. For he must first learn the nature of the good itself, and then pass on to apprehend that it is useful, and that it is choiceworthy for its own sake, and that it is productive of happiness. But that the aforesaid at- **175** tributes are not sufficient to indicate the concept and the real nature of the good is made plain by the practice of the dogmatists. All, probably, agree that the good is useful and that it is choiceworthy (so that the good is said to be, as it were, "the delightful") and that it is productive of happiness; but when asked what the thing is to which these properties belong, they plunge into a truceless war, some saying it is virtue, others pleasure, others painlessness, and others something else. And yet, if the essence of the good had been proved from the foregoing definitions, they would not have been at feud as though its nature were unknown.

176   Such, then, is the discord amongst those who are reputed the most eminent of the dogmatists regarding the notion of the good; and they have differed likewise regarding evil, some defining evil as "damage or not other than damage,"* others as "what is to be shunned for its own sake," others as "what is productive of unhappiness." But since they express by these phrases not the essence of evil but some of its possible attributes they are involved in the logical impasse mentioned above.

177   The term "indifferent," they say, is used in three senses—in one sense, of that which is an object of neither inclination nor disinclination, as for instance the fact that the stars or the hairs of the head are even in number; in another sense, of that which is an object of inclination or disinclination, but not towards this particular object any more than towards that, as in the case of two indistinguishable tetradrachms,† when one has to choose one of them; for there arises an inclination to choose one of them, but not this one more than that one; and a third sense of the term "indifferent" is, they say, "that which

---

*"Damage" or "harm" being the opposite of "utility" or "benefit"— the Stoic definition of "good."

†[An ancient Greek silver coin worth four drachmas.]

contributes neither to happiness nor to unhappiness," as health, or wealth; for what a man may use now well, now ill, that, they say, is indifferent, and they claim to discuss it specifically in their Ethics. But **178** what view we ought to take regarding this conception is plain from what we have already said about things good and evil.

Thus, then, it is plain that they have not guided us to a clear conception of the several things above-mentioned; yet, in thus failing with regard to matters that, perhaps, have no real existence, their experience is by no means strange. For there are some who argue on the following grounds that nothing is by nature either good or evil or indifferent.

CHAPTER XXIII. IS ANYTHING BY NATURE GOOD, BAD, OR INDIFFERENT?

Fire which heats by nature appears to all as heating, **179** and snow which chills by nature appears to all as chilling, and all things which move by nature move equally all those who are, as they say, in a natural condition. But none of the so-called "goods," as we shall show, moves all men as being good; therefore no natural good exists. And that none of the so-called goods moves all men alike is, they assert, an evident fact. For, not to mention ordinary folk— **180** of whom some regard right bodily condition as good, others chambering, others gluttony, others drunkenness, others gambling, others greed, and others still worse things,—some of the philosophers themselves (such as the Peripatetics) say that there are three kinds of goods; of these some concern the soul, like the virtues, others the body, like health and similar things, while others are external, such as friends, wealth, and

181 the like. The Stoics themselves, too, assert that there is a trinity of goods; of these some have to do with the soul, like the virtues, others are external, like the good man and the friend, while others are neither of the soul nor external, as for instance the good man in relation to himself; but they deny that the bodily states, which the Peripatetics declare to be goods, are goods. And some have accepted pleasure as a good, whereas some affirm that it is a downright evil, so that one professor of philosophy* actually exclaimed, "I would sooner be mad than merry."

182 If, then, things which move by nature move all men alike, while we are not all moved alike by the so-called goods, there is nothing good by nature. In fact is is impossible to believe either all the views now set forth, because of their conflicting character, or any one of them. For he who asserts that one must believe this view, but not that, becomes a party to the controversy, since he has opposed to him the arguments of those who take the rival view, and therefore he himself, along with the rest, will need an adjudicator instead of pronouncing judgment on others. And as there does not exist any agreed criterion or proof owing to the unsettled controversy about these matters, he will be reduced to suspending

---

*[Antisthenes (ca. 455–360 B.C.), a devoted follower of Socrates and reputed founder of the Cynic sect.]

judgment, and consequently he will be unable to affirm positively what the good by nature is.

Further, it is asserted by some that good is either **183** the choice itself or that which we choose. Now choice is not good according to its proper meaning; else we would not have been hurrying to obtain that which we choose, for fear of losing the power of continuing to choose it; for example, if the seeking to get drink were good, we would not have hurried to obtain drink; for when we have enjoyed it we are quit of seeking to get it. So, too, with hunger and love and the rest. Choice, then, is not choiceworthy in itself, even if it is not actually disagreeable; for in fact the hungry man hurries to partake of food in order to get quit of the discomfort due to his hunger; and so likewise the man in love and the thirsty man.

But neither is the good the choiceworthy. For **184** this is either external to us or in connection with us. But if it is external to us either it produces in us a soothing motion and a welcome condition and a delightful feeling, or it does not affect us at all. And if it is not a delight to us it will not be good, nor will it attract us to the choosing of it, nor will it be choiceworthy at all. And if there arises within us, from the external object, a congenial condition and an agreeable feeling, it is not for its own sake that the external object will be choiceworthy but for the sake of the internal condition which follows upon it; so that what is choiceworthy in itself cannot be **185** external. Nor can it be personal to us. For it is said to belong either to the body alone or to the soul alone or to both. But if it belongs to the body alone, it will elude our perception; for our perceptions are said to be properties of the soul, and they assert that the body, viewed by itself, is irrational. And if it should be said to extend to the soul also, it would seem to be choiceworthy owing to its affecting the soul and to the agreeable feeling therein; for, according to them, what is judged to be choiceworthy is judged by the intellect and not by the irrational body.

186 There remains the alternative that the good is in the soul only. But this, too, is impossible if we go by the statements of the dogmatists. For the soul is, perhaps, actually nonexistent; and even if it exists, judging by what they say it is not apprehended, as I have argued in my chapter "On the Criterion." How then could one venture to affirm that something takes

187 place in a thing which he does not apprehend? But, to pass over these objections, in what manner does the good, according to them, come about in the soul? For certainly, if Epicurus makes the end consist in pleasure and asserts that the soul, like all else, is composed of atoms, it is impossible to explain how in a heap of atoms there can come about pleasure and assent or judgment that this object is choiceworthy and good, that object to be avoided and evil.

CHAPTER XXIV. WHAT IS THE SO-CALLED ART
OF LIVING?

188 Again, the Stoics declare that goods of the soul are certain arts, namely the virtues. And an art, they say, is "a system composed of coexercised apprehensions,"* and the perceptions arise in the ruling principle. But how there takes place in the ruling principle, which according to them is breath, a deposit of perceptions, and such an aggregation of them as to produce art, it is impossible to conceive, when each succeeding impression obliterates the previous one, seeing that breath is fluid and it is said to move as a whole at each impression. For it is perfect **189** nonsense to say that Plato's imaginary construction of the soul—I mean the mixture of the indivisible and the divisible essence and of the nature of the other and of the same, or the numbers—is capable of being receptive of the good. Hence the good cannot **190** belong to the soul either. But if the good is not choice itself, and what is choiceworthy in itself neither exists externally nor belongs to either body or soul—as I have argued,—then there does not exist at all any natural good.

For the foregoing reasons also there exists no natural evil. For things which seem to some to be evil are pursued as goods by others—for instance, incontinence, injustice, avarice, intemperance, and the like. Hence, if it is the nature of things naturally existent to move all men alike, whereas the things said to be evil do not move all alike, nothing is naturally evil.

---

*The virtues, said the Stoics, are "arts" because they are forms of knowledge and consist in the use of "exercise" of a large number of perceptions or "apprehensions" related to one another in a systematic way. These "apprehensions" are "deposited" in the mind which is conceived as an elastic fluid pneuma [spirit, breath] of which the whole moves when any part of it is moved.

191   Similarly there is nothing naturally indifferent, because of the divergence of opinion about things indifferent. The Stoics, for example, assert that of the indifferents some are preferred, some rejected, and others neither preferred nor rejected,—the preferred being such as have sufficient value, like health and wealth; the rejected such as have not sufficient value, like poverty and sickness; while extending the finger or bending it in are cases of the neither preferred **192** nor rejected. Some, however, maintain that none of the indifferents is by nature preferred or rejected; for, owing to the differences in the circumstances, each of the indifferents appears at one time preferred, at another rejected. For certainly, they argue, if the rich were being threatened with attack by a tyrant while the poor were being left in peace, everyone would prefer to be poor rather than rich, so that wealth **193** would be a thing rejected. Consequently, since of each of the so-called indifferents some say that it is good, others bad, whereas all alike would have counted it indifferent had it been naturally indifferent, there is nothing that is naturally indifferent.

So also, should anyone declare that courage is naturally choiceworthy because lions seem to be naturally bold and courageous, bulls too, it may be, and some men and cocks, we reply that, as for that, cowardice also is one of the things naturally choiceworthy, since deer and hares and many other animals are naturally impelled thereto. The majority of men, too, show themselves to be cowardly; for it is rare for a man to give himself up to death for the sake of his country, or to seem inspired to do any other daring deed, the great majority of mankind being averse to all such actions.

Hence, also, the Epicureans suppose themselves **194** to have proved that pleasure is naturally choice-worthy; for the animals, they say, as soon as they are born, when still unperverted, seek after pleasure and avoid pains. But to these we may reply that **195** what is productive of evil cannot be naturally good; but pleasure is productive of evils; for to every pleasure there is linked a pain, and pain, according to them, is a natural evil. Thus, for example, the drunkard feels pleasure when filling himself with wine, and the glutton with food, and the lecher in immoderate sexual intercourse, yet these things are productive of both poverty and sickness, which, as they say, are painful and evil. Pleasure, therefore, is not a natural good. Similarly, too, what is productive of **196** good is not naturally evil, and pains bring about pleasures; it is, in fact, by toil that we acquire knowledge, and it is thus also that a man becomes possessed both of wealth and of his lady-love, and pains preserve health. Toil, then, is not naturally evil. Indeed if pleasure were naturally good, and toil bad, all men, as we said, would have been similarly disposed towards them, whereas we see many of the philosophers choosing toil and hardship and despising pleasure.

And so, too, those who assert that the virtuous **197** life is naturally good might be refuted by the fact that some of the sages choose the life which includes pleasure, so that the claim that a thing is by nature of this sort or that is contradicted by the divergence of opinion amongst the dogmatists themselves.

198   And perhaps it may not be amiss, in addition to what has been said, to dwell more in detail, though briefly, on the notions concerning things shameful and not shameful, unholy and not so, laws and customs, piety towards the gods, reverence for the departed, and the like. For thus we shall discover a great variety of belief concerning what ought or ought not to be done.

199   For example, amongst us* sodomy is regarded as shameful or rather illegal, but by the Germani,† they say, it is not looked on as shameful but as a customary thing. It is said, too, that in Thebes long ago this practice was not held to be shameful, and they say that Meriones the Cretan was so called by way of indicating the Cretans' custom,‡ and some refer to this the burning love of Achilles for Patro-
200 clus.§ And what wonder, when both the adherents of the Cynic philosophy and the followers of Zeno of Citium, Cleanthes** and Chrysippus, declare that this practice is indifferent? Having intercourse with a woman, too, in public, although deemed by us to be shameful, is not thought to be shameful by some of the Indians; at any rate they couple publicly

---

*"Amongst us" here, and throughout this chapter, means "amongst the Greeks" and refers in special to the laws or customs of Athens.

†Prob. not "Germans," but a Persian tribe.

‡ The name Meriones is derived from [the Greek word] *mêros* ("thigh").

§ Plato, *Symposium*, 180a.

**[331–232 B.C. Succeeded Zeno of Citium as head of the Stoic school from 263 to 232.]

with indifference, like the philosopher Crates, as the story goes. Moreover, prostitution is with us a shameful and disgraceful thing, but with many of the Egyptians it is highly esteemed; at least, they say that those women who have the greatest number of lovers wear an ornamental ankle ring as a token of their proud position. And with some of them the girls marry after collecting a dowry before marriage by means of prostitution. We see the Stoics declaring that it is not amiss to keep company with a prostitute or to live on the profits of prostitution. **201**

Moreover, with us tattooing is held to be shameful and degrading, but many of the Egyptians and Sarmatians tattoo their offspring. Also, it is a shameful thing with us for men to wear earrings, but amongst some of the barbarians, like the Syrians, it is a token of nobility. And some, by way of marking their nobility still further, pierce the nostrils also of their children and suspend from them rings of silver or gold—a thing which nobody with us would do, just as no man here would dress himself in a flowered robe reaching to the feet, although this dress, which with us is thought shameful, is held to be highly respectable by the Persians. And when, at the court of Dionysius the tyrant of Sicily, a dress of this description was offered to the philosophers Plato and Aristippus, Plato sent it away with the words— **202 203 204**

A man am I, and never could I don
A woman's garb;

but Aristippus accepted it, saying—

> For e'en midst revel-routs
> She that is chaste will keep her purity.

205 Thus, even in the case of these sages, while the one of them deemed this practice shameful, the other did not. And with us it is sinful to marry one's mother or one's own sister; but the Persians, and especially those of them who are reputed to practice wisdom— namely, the Magi,—marry their mothers; and the Egyptians take their sisters in marriage, even as the poet says*—

> Thus spake Zeus unto Hera, his wedded wife and his sister.

206 Moreover, Zeno of Citium says that it is not amiss for a man to rub his mother's private part with his own private part, just as no one would say it was bad for him to rub any other part of her body with his hand. Chrysippus, too, in his book *The State* approves of a father getting children by his daughter, a mother by her son, and a brother by his sister. And Plato,† in more general terms, has declared that wives ought to be held in common. Masturbation, too, which we count loathsome, is not disapproved by Zeno; and we are informed that others, too, practice this evil as though it were a good thing.

---

*Homer, *Iliad*, xviii. 356.
† *Republic*, v. 457.

Moreover, the eating of human flesh is sinful **207** with us, but indifferent amongst whole tribes of barbarians. Yet why should one speak of "barbarians" when even Tydeus* is said to have devoured the brains of his enemy, and the Stoic school declare that it is not wrong for a man to eat either other men's flesh or his own? And with most of us it is sinful **208** to defile an altar of a god with human blood, but the Laconians lash themselves fiercely over the altar of Artemis Orthosia† in order that a great stream of blood may flow over the altar of the goddess. Moreover, some sacrifice a human victim to Cronos, just as the Scythians sacrifice strangers to Artemis; whereas we deem that holy places are defiled by the slaying of a man. Adulterers are, of course, punished **209** by law with us, but amongst some peoples intercourse with other men's wives is a thing indifferent; and some philosophers,‡ too, declare that intercourse with the wife of another is indifferent.

With us, also, the law enjoins that the fathers **210** should receive due care from their children; but the Scythians cut their throats when they get to be over sixty years old. And what wonder, seeing that Cronos cut off his father's genitals with a sickle, and Zeus plunged Cronos down to Tartarus, and Athena with the help of Hera and Poseidon attempted to bind her father with fetters? Moreover, Cronos decided **211**

---

*Tydeus, father of Diomede; his "enemy" was Melanippus (*Iliad,* xiv. 144 ff.).
†Boys were scourged at the altar of Artemis Orthia in Laconia.
‡E.g., Diogenes the Cynic.

to destroy his own children, and Solon* gave the Athenians the law "concerning things immune," by which he allowed each man to slay his own child; but with us the laws forbid the slaying of children. The Roman lawgivers also ordain that the children are subjects and slaves of their fathers, and that power over the children's property belongs to the fathers and not the children, until the children have obtained their freedom like bought slaves; but this custom is

212 rejected by others as being despotic. It is the law, too, that homicide should be punished; but gladiators when they kill often receive actual commendation. Moreover, the laws prevent the striking of free men; yet when athletes strike free men, and often even kill them, they are deemed worthy of rewards and

213 crowns. With us, too, the law bids each man to have one wife, but amongst the Thracians and Gaetulians (a Libyan tribe) each man has many wives. Piracy,

214 too, is with us illegal and criminal, but with many of the barbarians it is not disapproved. Indeed they say that the Cilicians used to regard it as a noble pursuit, so that they held those who died in the course of piracy to be worthy of honor. So too Nestor— in the poet's account†—after welcoming Telemachus and his comrades, addresses them thus—

> Say, are you roaming
> Aimlessly, like sea-rovers?

---

*[Athenian statesman and poet (ca. 640–560 B.C.).]
†Homer, *Odyssey,* iii. 73.

Yet, if piracy had been an improper thing, he would not have welcomed them in this friendly way, because of his suspicion that they might be people of that kind.

Moreover, thieving is with us illegal and criminal; **215** yet those who declare that Hermes is a most thievish god cause this practice to be accounted not criminal— for how could a god be bad? And some say that the Laconians also punished those who thieved, not because they had thieved, but because they had been found out. Moreover, the coward and the man who **216** throws away his shield are in many places punished by law; and this is why the Laconian mother, when giving a shield to her son as he set out for the war, said, "Either with this, my child, or upon it." Yet Archilochus,* as though vaunting to us of his flight after flinging away his shield, speaks thus of himself in his poems—

> Over my shield some Saïan warrior gloats,—
> The shield I left, though loth, beside the bush—
> A flawless piece of armor; I myself
> Fled and escaped from death which endeth all.

And the Amazons used to maim the males amongst **217** their offspring so as to make them incapable of any manly action, while they themselves attended to warfare; though with us the opposite practice is regarded as right. The Mother of the gods,† also, ap-

---

*[Greek iambic poet from the island of Paros (fl. ca. 680 B.C.).]
†Cybele, whose priests were eunuchs.

218 proves of effeminates, and the goddess would not have decided thus if unmanliness were naturally a bad thing. So it is that, in regard to justice and injustice and the excellence of manliness, there is a great variety of opinion.

Around all matters of religion and theology also, there rages violent controversy. For while the majority declare that gods exist, some deny their existence, like Diagoras of Melos, and Theodorus, and Critias the Athenian.* And of those who maintain the existence of gods, some believe in the ancestral gods, others in such as are constructed in the dogmatic systems—as Aristotle asserted that God is incorporeal and "the limit of heaven," the Stoics that he is a breath which permeates even through things foul, Epicurus that he is anthropomorphic, Xenophanes **219** that he is an impassive sphere. Some, too, hold that he cares for human affairs, others that he does not so care; for Epicurus declares that "what is blessed and incorruptible neither feels trouble itself nor causes it to others." Hence ordinary people differ also, some saying that there is one god, others that there are many gods and of various shapes; in fact, they even come to share the notions of the Egyptians who believe in gods that are dog-faced, or hawk-shaped, or cows or crocodiles or anything else.

220 Hence, too, sacrificial usages, and the ritual of worship in general, exhibit great diversity. For things

---

*Diagoras, atomist and poet, ca. 420 B.C.; Theodorus, a Cyrenaic, ca. 310 B.C.; Critias, orator and poet, one of the "Thirty Tyrants" (404 B.C.) of Athens.

which are in some cults accounted holy are in others accounted unholy. But this would not have been so if the holy and the unholy existed by nature. Thus, for example, no one would sacrifice a pig to Sarapis, but they sacrifice it to Heracles and Asclepius. To sacrifice a sheep to Isis is forbidden, but it is offered up in honor of the so-called Mother of the gods and of other deities. To Cronos a human victim is **221** sacrificed at Carthage, although this is regarded by most as an impious act. In Alexandria they offer a cat to Horus and a beetle to Thetis—a thing which no one here would do. To Poseidon they sacrifice a horse; but to Apollo (especially the Didymaean* Apollo) that animal is an abomination. It is an act of piety to offer goats to Artemis, but not to Asclepius. And I might add a host of similar instances, but **222** I forbear since my aim is to be brief. Yet surely, if a sacrifice had been holy by nature or unholy, it would have been deemed so by all men alike.

Examples similar to these may also be found in the religious observances with regard to human diet. For a Jew or an Egyptian priest would sooner **223** die than eat swine's flesh; by a Libyan it is regarded as a most impious thing to taste the meat of a sheep, by some of the Syrians to eat a dove, and by others to eat sacrificial victims. And in certain cults it is lawful, but in others impious, to eat fish. And amongst the Egyptians some of those who are reputed to be sages believe it is sinful to eat an animal's head, others

---

*I.e., of Didymus, near Miletus.

the shoulder, others the foot, others some other part.
224 And no one would bring an onion as an offering
to Zeus Casius of Pelusium,* just as no priest of
the Libyan Aphrodite would taste garlic. And in some
cults they abstain from mint, in others from catmint,
in others from parsley. And some declare that they
would sooner eat their fathers' heads than beans.†
225 Yet, amongst others, these things are indifferent.
Eating dog's flesh, too, is thought by us to be sinful,
but some of the Thracians are reported to be dog-
eaters. Possibly this practice was customary also
amongst the Greeks; and on this account Diocles,
too, starting from the practices of the Asclepiadae,‡
prescribes that hounds' flesh should be given to certain patients. And some, as I have said, even eat
human flesh indifferently, a thing which with us is
226 accounted sinful. Yet, if the rules of ritual and of
unlawful foods had existed by nature, they would
have been observed by all men alike.

A similar account may be given of reverence
towards the departed. Some wrap the dead up completely and then cover them with earth, thinking that
it is impious to expose them to the sun; but the
Egyptians take out their entrails and embalm them
and keep them above ground with themselves. The
227 fish-eating tribes of the Ethiopians cast them into the
lakes, there to be devoured by the fish; the Hyrcanians§

---

*East of the Nile delta.
†Probably a Pythagorean (or Orphic) taboo.
‡The earliest Greek medical guild; Diocles was a famous physician of
the fourth century B.C.
§[Who lived] south of the Caspian Sea.

expose them as prey to dogs, and some of the Indians to vultures. And they say that some of the Troglodytes* take the corpse to a hill, and then after tying its head to its feet cast stones upon it amidst laughter, and when they have made a heap of stones over it they leave it there. And some of the barbarians slay and **228** eat those who are over sixty years old, but bury in the earth those who die young. Some burn the dead; and of these some recover and preserve their bones, while others show no care but leave them scattered about. And they say that the Persians impale their dead and embalm them with niter, after which they wrap them round in bandages. How much grief others endure for the dead we see ourselves.

Some, too, believe death itself to be dreadful **229** and horrible, others do not. Thus Euripides says:

> Who knows if life be but the state of death,
> And death be counted life in realms below?

And Epicurus declares: "Death is nothing to us; for what is dissolved is senseless, and what is senseless is nothing to us." They also declare that, inasmuch as we are compounded of soul and body, and death is a dissolution of soul and body, when we exist death does not exist (for we are not being dissolved), and when death exists we do not exist, for through the cessation of the compound of soul and body we too cease to exist. And Heracleitus states that both life **230** and death exist both in our state of life and in our

---

*Cave-dwellers of the west coast of the Red Sea [south of Egypt].

state of death; for when we live our souls are dead and buried within us, and when we die our souls revive and live. And some even suppose that dying is better for us than living. Thus Euripides says:

> Rather should we assemble to bewail
> The babe new-born, such ills has he to face;
> Whereas the dead, who has surcease from woe,
> With joy and gladness we should bear from home.

231 These lines,* too, spring from the same sentiment:

> Not to have been begotten at all were the best thing
> for mortals,
> Nor to have looked upon fiery rays of the sun;
> Or, if begotten, to hasten amain to the portals of Hades,
> And to lie unmoved robed in masses of earth.

We know, too, the facts about Cleobis and Biton which Herodotus relates in his story of the Argive **232** priestess. It is reported, also, that some of the Thracians sit round the newborn babe and chant dirges. So, then, death should not be considered a thing naturally dreadful, just as life should not be considered a thing naturally good. Thus none of the things mentioned above is naturally of this character or of that, but all are matters of convention and relative.

233 The same method of treatment may be applied also to each of the other customs, which we have not now described owing to the summary character

---

*Theognis, 425 ff.

of our exposition. And even if, in regard to some of them, we are unable to declare their discrepancy offhand, we ought to observe that disagreement concerning them may possibly exist amongst certain nations that are unknown to us. For just as, if we **234** had been ignorant, say, of the custom amongst the Egyptians of marrying sisters, we should have asserted wrongly that it was universally agreed that men ought not to marry sisters,—even so, in regard to those practices wherein we notice no discrepancy, it is not proper for us to affirm that there is no disagreement about them, since, as I said, disagreement about them may possibly exist amongst some of the nations which are unknown to us.

Accordingly, the skeptic, seeing so great a di- **235** versity of usages, suspends judgment as to the natural existence of anything good or bad or (in general) fit or unfit to be done, therein abstaining from the rashness of dogmatism; and he follows undogmatically the ordinary rules of life, and because of this he remains impassive in respect of matters of opinion, while in conditions that are necessitated his emotions are moderate; for though, as a human being, he suffers **236** emotion through his senses, yet because he does not also opine that what he suffers is evil by nature, the emotion he suffers is moderate. For the added opinion that a thing itself is of such a kind is worse than the actual suffering itself, just as sometimes the patients themselves bear a surgical operation, while the bystanders swoon away because of their opinion that it is a horrible experience. But, in fact, he who assumes **237** that there exists by nature something good or bad or, generally, fit or unfit to be done, is disquieted in various ways. For when he experiences what he regards as natural evils he deems himself to be pursued by Furies, and when he becomes possessed of what seems to him good things he falls into no ordinary state of disquiet both through arrogance and through fear of losing them, and through trying to guard against finding himself again amongst what he regards **238** as natural evils; for those who assert that goods are incapable of being lost* we shall put to silence by means of the doubts raised by their dissension. Hence we conclude that if what is productive of evil is evil and to be shunned, and the persuasion that these things are good, those evil, by nature produces disquiet, then the assumption and persuasion that anything is, in its real nature, either bad or good is evil and to be shunned.

For the present, then, this account of things good, evil, and indifferent is sufficient.

CHAPTER XXV. DOES THERE EXIST AN ART OF LIVING?

239 It is plain from what has been said above that there can be no art of living. For if such an art exists, it has to do with the consideration of things good, evil, and indifferent, so that these being nonexistent the art of living also is nonexistent. Further, since

---

*The Cynics and some Stoics.

the dogmatists do not all with one accord lay down one single art of living, but some propound one art, some another, they are guilty of discrepancy and open to the argument from discrepancy which I stated in our discussion of the good. Yet, even if they were **240** all to agree in assuming that the art of living is one— such as, for example, the celebrated "prudence"' whereof the Stoics dream, and which seems to be more convincing than all the rest,—even so equally absurd results will follow. For since "prudence" is a virtue, and the sage alone was in possession of virtue, the Stoics, not being sages, will not be in possession of the art of living. And in general, since, according to **241** them, no art can have real existence, an art of living cannot exist, so far as their statements go.

Thus, for example, they declare that art is "a composite of apprehensions," and apprehension is "assent to an apprehensive impression." But the apprehensive impression is indiscoverable; for every impression is not apprehensive, nor is it possible to decide which one of the impressions is the apprehensive impression, since we cannot simply decide by means of every impression which one is apprehensive and which not, while if we require an apprehensive impression in order to determine which is the apprehensive impression we are wrecked on the *ad infinitum* fallacy, since we are asking for another apprehensive impression so as to determine the impression taken to be apprehensive. And herein, **242** too, the procedure of the Stoics, in presenting the notion of the apprehensive impression, is logically unsound; for in stating, on the one hand, that an apprehensive impression is that which is derived from a real object, and, on the other hand, that a real object is that which is capable of giving rise to an apprehensive impression, they fall into the fallacy of circular reasoning. If, then, in order that an art of living may exist, there must first exist art, and in order that art may subsist apprehension must pre-exist, and in order that apprehension may subsist assent to an apprehensive impression must be apprehended, but the apprehensive impression is indiscoverable,—then the art of living is indiscoverable.

243 Another argument is this. Every art appears to be apprehended by means of its own special products, but there is no special product of the art of living; for anything you might mention as its product—such as honoring parents, paying back deposits, and all the rest—is found to be common to ordinary folk as well. Therefore no art of living exists. For we shall not ascertain (as some assert) from the apparent derivation of some speech or operation of the prudent man from a state of prudence that is a product of **244** prudence. For the state of prudence itself is inapprehensible, not being directly apparent either of itself or from its products, these being common to ordinary folk as well. And to say that we apprehend the possessor of the art of living by the unvarying quality of his actions is the assertion of those who overestimate human nature and are visionaries rather than truth-tellers:

As is the day which upon them is brought by the
    sire immortal,
So are the minds of mortal men.*

There remains the assertion that the art of living **245**
is apprehended by means of those effects which they
describe in their books; and these being numerous
and much alike, I will extract a few of them by way
of examples. Thus, for instance, Zeno, the master
of their sect, in his treatises, amongst many other
statements regarding the rearing of children, says this:
"Have carnal knowledge no less and no more of a
favorite than of a nonfavorite child, nor of a female
than of a male; favorite or nonfavorite, males or
females, no different conduct, but the same, befits
and is befitting to all alike." And as concerns piety **246**
towards parents, the same man states, in reference
to the story of Jocasta and Oedipus, that there was
nothing dreadful in his rubbing his mother: "If she
had been ailing in one part of her body and he had
done her good by rubbing it with his hands, it had
not been shameful; was it, then, shameful for him
to stop her grief and give her joy by rubbing other
parts, and to beget noble children by his mother?"
And with this opinion Chrysippus also agrees. At
least he says in his *State:* "I approve of carrying out
those practices—which, quite rightly, are customary
even nowadays amongst many peoples—according
to which a mother has children by her son, the father
by his daughter, the brother by his full sister." And **247**

Odyssey, xviii. 136-137.

he proceeds, in the same treatises, to introduce amongst us cannibalism, saying: "And if from a living body a part be cut off that is good for food, we should not bury it nor otherwise get rid of it, but consume it, so that from our parts a new part may **248** arise." And in his book *On Duty* he says expressly, regarding the burial of parents: "When our parents decease we should use the simplest forms of burial, as though the body—like the nails or teeth or hair— were nothing to us, and we need bestow no care or attention on a thing like it. Hence, also, men should make use of the flesh, when it is good, for food, just as also when one of their own parts, such as the foot, is cut off, it would be proper that it and the like parts should be so used; but when the flesh is not good, they should either bury it and leave it, or burn it up and let the ashes lie, or cast it far away and pay no more regard to it than to nails or hair."

249   Of such a kind are most of the philosophers' theories; but they would not dare to put them into practice unless they lived under the laws of the Cyclopes or Laestrygones.* But if they are totally incapable of acting thus, and their actual conduct is common to ordinary folk as well, there is no action peculiar to those who are suspected of possessing the art of living. So then, if the arts must certainly be apprehended by means of their peculiar effects, and no effect is observed that is peculiar to the so-

*[A race of giant cannibals encountered by Odysseus.]

called art of living, this art is not apprehended. Consequently, no one can positively affirm regarding it that it is really existent.

Chapter XXVI. Does the Art of Living arise in Mankind?

Moreover, if the art of living comes into existence **250** in men, it so comes either by nature or through learning and teaching. But if it is by nature, then the art of living will arise in them either in so far as they are men, or in so far as they are not men. Certainly not in so far as they are not men; for it is not a fact that they are not men. But if it is in so far as they are men, then prudence would have belonged to all men, so that all would have been prudent and virtuous and wise. But they describe most men as bad. Neither, then, in so far as they **251** are men will the art of living belong to them. Therefore it does not accrue by nature. And again, since they insist that art is "a system of coexercised apprehensions," they make it evident that the art under discussion, as well as all other arts, is acquired rather by some sort of effort and learning.

Chapter XXVII. Is the Art of Living capable of being taught?

But neither is it acquired by teaching and learning. **252** For in order that these should subsist, three things must first be agreed upon—the matter which is being taught, the teacher and the learner, and the method of learning. But none of these subsists; neither, then, does teaching.

CHAPTER XXVIII. DOES A MATTER OF INSTRUCTION EXIST?

253 Thus, for instance, the matter of instruction is either true or false; if false it would not be taught; for they assert that falsehood is nonexistent, and of nonexistents there could be no teaching. Nor yet if it were said to be true; for we have shown in our chapter "On the Criterion" that truth is nonexistent. If, then, neither the false nor the true is being taught, and besides these there is nothing capable of being taught (for no one, to be sure, will say that, though these are unteachable, he teaches only dubious lessons), then nothing **254** is taught. And the matter taught is either apparent or nonevident. But if it is apparent, it will not require teaching; for things apparent appear to all alike. And if it is nonevident, then, since things nonevident are, as we have often shown, inapprehensible owing to the undecided controversy about them, it will be incapable of being taught; for how could anyone teach or learn what he does not apprehend? But if neither the apparent is taught nor the nonevident, nothing is taught.

255 Again, what is taught is either corporeal or incorporeal, and each of these being either apparent or nonevident is incapable of being taught, according to the argument we have just now stated. Nothing, therefore, is taught.

Further, either the existent is taught or the non- **256**
existent. Now the nonexistent is not taught; for if
the nonexistent is taught the nonexistent will be true,
since teaching is held to be of things true. And if
it is true, it will also subsist; for they declare that
"a true thing is what subsists and is opposed to
something." But it is absurd to say that the nonexistent subsists; therefore the nonexistent is not
taught. Yet neither is the existent. For if the existent **257**
is taught, it is taught either in so far as it is existent
or in so far as it is something else. But if it is to
be taught in so far as it is existent, it will be one
of the existing things, and therefore a thing incapable
of being taught; for teaching ought to proceed from
certain acknowledged facts which require no teaching. Therefore the existent, in so far as it is existent,
is not capable of being taught. Nor, in fact, in so
far as it is something else. For the existent has not
anything else which is nonexistent attached to it, so **258**
that if the existent in so far as it is existent is not
taught, neither will it be taught in so far as it is
something else; for whatsoever thing is attached to
it is existent. And further, whether the existent thing
which, they will say, is taught be apparent or nonevident, as it is subject to the absurdities we have
stated, it will be incapable of being taught. But if
neither the existent nor the nonexistent is taught, there
is nothing that is taught.

CHAPTER XXIX. DO THE TEACHER AND THE LEARNER EXIST?

259 Now with the refutation of this is involved that of both the teacher and the learner; though they are just as much open to doubt on their own account. For either the expert artist teaches the expert, or the nonexpert the nonexpert, or the nonexpert the expert, or the expert the nonexpert. Now the expert does not teach the expert; for neither of them, *qua* expert, needs teaching. Nor does the nonexpert teach the nonexpert, any more than the blind can lead the blind. Nor the nonexpert the expert, for it would **260** be ridiculous. The only thing left is to say that the expert teaches the nonexpert; and this, too, is a thing impossible. For it is declared to be wholly impossible that an expert artist should exist, since neither do we see anyone existing spontaneously and from birth as an expert, nor does anyone turn into an expert from being a nonexpert. For either one lesson and one apprehension can make an expert of the non-**261** expert or they cannot do so at all. But if one apprehension makes the nonexpert an expert, it will be open to us to declare, firstly, that art is not a system of apprehensions; for the man who knows nothing at all would be termed an expert if only he were taught a single lesson of art. And, secondly, should anyone assert that, as soon as a man who has acquired some principles of art and still needs one more, and because of this is nonexpert, acquires also that one principle, he at once becomes an expert instead of a nonexpert by means of one apprehension, he will **262** be making a random assertion. For in the case of individual men we could not point to one who, being still a nonexpert, will become an expert by acquiring one additional principle; for no one, to be sure, has such a command of the numeration of the principles of each art as to be able to say, by numbering off the known principles, how many are still needed to make up the full number of the principles of the art. So then the learning of one principle does not make the nonexpert an expert. But if this is true, **263** seeing that no one acquires all the principles of the arts at once, but each one singly, if at all—this point also being granted by way of assumption—the man who is said to acquire the principles of the art one by one will not be termed an expert; for we recall the conclusion that the learning of one principle cannot make an expert of the nonexpert. No one, then, becomes an expert from being a nonexpert. Hence, on these grounds too, the expert artist appears to be nonexistent. And therefore the teacher also.

Neither can the so-called learner, if he is non- **264** expert, learn and apprehend the principles of the art wherein he is nonexpert. For just as the man who is blind from birth, in so far as he is blind, will not acquire perception of colors, nor, similarly, he who is deaf from birth, of sound, so too the nonexpert will not apprehend the principles of the art wherein he is nonexpert. For should he do so the same man would be both expert and nonexpert in the same things—nonexpert since he is such by hypothesis, and

265 expert since he has apprehension of the principles of the art. Hence, neither does the expert teach the nonexpert. But if neither the expert teaches the expert, nor the nonexpert the nonexpert, nor the nonexpert the expert, nor the expert the nonexpert, and these are all the alternatives possible, then neither the teacher exists nor the taught.

CHAPTER XXX. DOES THERE EXIST ANY METHOD OF LEARNING?

266 And if neither the learner nor the teacher exists, the method of teaching also is abolished. And it is no less disputed on the following grounds. The method of teaching comes to exist either by ocular evidence or by speech; but it does not come to exist either by ocular evidence or by speech, as we shall show; therefore the method of learning also is not easy to discover.

Now teaching does not come by ocular evidence, since ocular evidence consists in things exhibited. But what is exhibited is apparent to all; and the apparent, *qua* apparent, is perceptible by all; and what is perceptible by all in common is incapable of being taught; therefore nothing is capable of being taught by ocular evidence.

267 Nor, in fact, is anything taught by speech. For speech either signifies something or signifies nothing. But if it signifies nothing, neither will it be capable of teaching anything. And if it signifies something, it does so either by nature or by convention. But

it is not significant by nature because all men do not understand all when they hear them, as is the case with Greeks hearing barbarians talk or barbarians hearing Greeks. And if it is significant by **268** convention, evidently those who have grasped beforehand the objects to which the several words are assigned will perceive those objects, not through being taught by the words things of which they were ignorant, but by recollecting and recovering things which they knew; whereas those who require to learn what they do not know, and who are ignorant of the objects to which the words are assigned, will have no perception of anything. Consequently, the method **269** of learning also will be incapable of subsisting. For, in fact, the teacher ought to impart to the learner an apprehension of the principles of the art he is teaching, so that the latter by apprehending them as a system may thus become an expert artist. But, as we have shown above, apprehension is nothing; therefore also the method of teaching cannot subsist. But if neither the matter taught exists, nor the teacher and the learner, nor the method of learning, then neither learning exists nor teaching.

Such, then, are the objections put forward re- **270** garding learning and teaching in general. And the same difficulties may also be alleged in the case of the so-called art of living. Thus, for instance, we have shown above that the matter taught, namely prudence, is nonexistent; and both the teacher and the learner are nonexistent. For either the prudent man will teach the prudent the art of living, or the imprudent the imprudent, or the imprudent the prudent, or the prudent the imprudent; but none of these teaches any other; therefore the so-called art

271 of living is not taught. Probably it is superfluous even to refer to the other cases; but if the prudent man teaches prudence to the imprudent, and prudence is "knowledge of things good and evil and neither," the imprudent man, as he does not possess prudence, possesses ignorance of the things that are good and evil and neither; and since he possesses nothing but ignorance thereof, when the prudent man teaches him what things are good and evil and neither, he will merely hear what is said and will not get to know the things. For if he should grasp them while in a state of imprudence, then imprudence too will be capable of perceiving what things are good and evil

272 and neither. But, according to them, imprudence is certainly not capable of perceiving these things, since, if it were, the imprudent man will be prudent. Therefore, according to the definition of prudence, the imprudent man does not grasp what is said or done by the prudent. And, as he fails to grasp, he will not be taught by him, especially since, as we have said above, he cannot be taught either by ocular evidence or by means of speech. But, in fine, if the so-called art of living is not imparted to anyone either by means of learning and teaching or by nature, then the art of living, so harped on by the philosophers, is indiscoverable.

273 Yet even were one to grant, as an act of bounty, that this visionary art of living is imparted to someone, it will show itself to be hurtful to its possessors, and a cause of perturbation, rather than beneficial.

Chapter XXXI. Does the Art of Living benefit its Possessor?

Thus, for instance—to take a few arguments out of many by way of example—the art of living might be thought to benefit the wise man by furnishing him with temperance in his impulses towards good and repulsions from evil. He, then, who is termed **274** by them a temperate sage is called temperate either in virtue of his never feeling the impulse towards good or repulsion from evil, or in virtue of his possessing slight impulses in either direction and overcoming them by reason. But in respect of his freedom **275** from bad resolutions he will not be self-controlled; for he will not control what he does not possess. And just as one would not call a eunuch temperate in sex-indulgence, or a man with a poor stomach temperate in respect of the pleasures of the table (for they feel no attraction at all towards such things, so that they might rise superior to the attraction through temperance),—in the same way we ought not to term the sage temperate, because he possesses no natural feeling over which he may exercise control. And if they shall claim that he is temperate in virtue **276** of his forming bad resolutions but overcoming them by reason, then, firstly, they will be admitting that prudence was of no benefit to him just when he was in a state of perturbation and needed assistance, and, secondly, he is found to be even more unfortunate than those they term bad. For if he feels an impulse towards anything, he is certainly perturbed; while if he overcomes it by reason, he retains the evil, and because of this he is more perturbed than the bad man who no longer experiences this feeling; for the

277 latter, though he is perturbed if he is feeling an impulse, yet ceases from this perturbation if he gains his desires.

So, then, the sage does not become temperate in virtue of his prudence; or if he does become so, he is of all men the most miserable, so that the art of living has brought him no benefit but the uttermost perturbation. And we have shown above that the man who believes that he possesses the art of living, and that by means of it he discerns what things are naturally good and what bad, is extremely perturbed both when

278 good things are his and when evil things. We must, then, declare that, if there is no agreement as to the existence of things good and bad and indifferent, and the art of living is possibly nonexistent, or—if its existence is provisionally admitted—brings no benefit to its possessors but, on the contrary, causes them extreme perturbations, then the dogmatists would seem to be vainly puffed up in respect of the so-called ethical division of what they term "philosophy."

279 Having now treated of the subject of ethics also at sufficient length for an account in outline, we conclude at this point our third book, and with it the complete treatise on "Pyrrhonean Outlines," adding only this final section:

Chapter XXXII. Why the Skeptic sometimes purposely propounds Arguments which are lacking in Power of Persuasion

The skeptic, being a lover of his kind, desires to cure **280** by speech, as best he can, the self-conceit and rashness of the dogmatists. So, just as the physicians who cure bodily ailments have remedies which differ in strength, and apply the severe ones to those whose ailments are severe and the milder to those mildly affected,—so too the skeptic propounds arguments which differ in strength, and employs those which **281** are weighty and capable by their stringency of disposing of the dogmatists' ailment, self-conceit, in cases where the mischief is due to a severe attack of rashness, while he employs the milder arguments in the case of those whose ailment of conceit is superficial and easy to cure, and whom it is possible to restore to health by milder methods of persuasion. Hence the adherent of skeptic principles does not scruple to propound at one time arguments that are weighty in their persuasiveness, and at another time such as appear less impressive,—and he does so on purpose, as the latter are frequently sufficient to enable him to effect his object.

GREAT BOOKS IN PHILOSOPHY PAPERBACK SERIES

ESTHETICS

❏ Aristotle—*The Poetics*
❏ Aristotle—*Treatise on Rhetoric*

ETHICS

❏ Aristotle—*The Nicomachean Ethics*
❏ Marcus Aurelius—*Meditations*
❏ Jeremy Bentham—*The Principles of Morals and Legislation*
❏ John Dewey—*Human Nature and Conduct*
❏ John Dewey—*The Moral Writings of John Dewey, Revised Edition*
❏ Epictetus—*Enchiridion*
❏ David Hume—*An Enquiry Concerning the Principles of Morals*
❏ Immanuel Kant—*Fundamental Principles of the Metaphysic of Morals*
❏ John Stuart Mill—*Utilitarianism*
❏ George Edward Moore—*Principia Ethica*
❏ Friedrich Nietzsche—*Beyond Good and Evil*
❏ Plato—*Protagoras, Philebus, and Gorgias*
❏ Bertrand Russell—*Bertrand Russell On Ethics, Sex, and Marriage*
❏ Arthur Schopenhauer—*The Wisdom of Life* and *Counsels and Maxims*
❏ Adam Smith—*The Theory of Moral Sentiments*
❏ Benedict de Spinoza—*Ethics* and *The Improvement of the Understanding*

LOGIC

❏ George Boole—*The Laws of Thought*

METAPHYSICS/EPISTEMOLOGY

❏ Aristotle—*De Anima*
❏ Aristotle—*The Metaphysics*
❏ Francis Bacon—*Essays*
❏ George Berkeley—*Three Dialogues Between Hylas and Philonous*
❏ W. K. Clifford—*The Ethics of Belief and Other Essays*
❏ René Descartes—*Discourse on Method* and *The Meditations*
❏ John Dewey—*How We Think*
❏ John Dewey—*The Influence of Darwin on Philosophy and Other Essays*
❏ Epicurus—*The Essential Epicurus: Letters, Principal Doctrines,*
      Vatican Sayings, and Fragments
❏ Sidney Hook—*The Quest for Being*
❏ David Hume—*An Enquiry Concerning Human Understanding*
❏ David Hume—*A Treatise on Human Nature*
❏ William James—*The Meaning of Truth*
❏ William James—*Pragmatism*
❏ Immanuel Kant—*The Critique of Judgment*
❏ Immanuel Kant—*Critique of Practical Reason*
❏ Immanuel Kant—*Critique of Pure Reason*
❏ Gottfried Wilhelm Leibniz—*Discourse on Metaphysics* and *The Monadology*
❏ John Locke—*An Essay Concerning Human Understanding*
❏ George Herbert Mead—*The Philosophy of the Present*

- ❏ Charles S. Peirce—*The Essential Writings*
- ❏ Plato—*The Euthyphro, Apology, Crito,* and *Phaedo*
- ❏ Plato—*Lysis, Phaedrus,* and *Symposium*
- ❏ Bertrand Russell—*The Problems of Philosophy*
- ❏ George Santayana—*The Life of Reason*
- ❏ Sextus Empiricus—*Outlines of Pyrrhonism*
- ❏ Ludwig Wittgenstein—*Wittgenstein's Lectures: Cambridge, 1932–1935*

PHILOSOPHY OF RELIGION

- ❏ Jeremy Bentham—*The Influence of Natural Religion on the Temporal Happiness of Mankind*
- ❏ Marcus Tullius Cicero—*The Nature of the Gods* and *On Divination*
- ❏ Ludwig Feuerbach—*The Essence of Christianity*
- ❏ Paul Henri Thiry, Baron d'Holbach—*Good Sense*
- ❏ David Hume—*Dialogues Concerning Natural Religion*
- ❏ William James—*The Varieties of Religious Experience*
- ❏ John Locke—*A Letter Concerning Toleration*
- ❏ Lucretius—*On the Nature of Things*
- ❏ John Stuart Mill—*Three Essays on Religion*
- ❏ Friedrich Nietzsche—*The Antichrist*
- ❏ Thomas Paine—*The Age of Reason*
- ❏ Bertrand Russell—*Bertrand Russell On God and Religion*

SOCIAL AND POLITICAL PHILOSOPHY

- ❏ Aristotle—*The Politics*
- ❏ Mikhail Bakunin—*The Basic Bakunin: Writings, 1869–1871*
- ❏ Edmund Burke—*Reflections on the Revolution in France*
- ❏ John Dewey—*Freedom and Culture*
- ❏ John Dewey—*Individualism Old and New*
- ❏ John Dewey—*Liberalism and Social Action*
- ❏ G. W. F. Hegel—*The Philosophy of History*
- ❏ G. W. F. Hegel—*Philosophy of Right*
- ❏ Thomas Hobbes—*The Leviathan*
- ❏ Sidney Hook—*Paradoxes of Freedom*
- ❏ Sidney Hook—*Reason, Social Myths, and Democracy*
- ❏ John Locke—*The Second Treatise on Civil Government*
- ❏ Niccolo Machiavelli—*The Prince*
- ❏ Karl Marx (with Friedrich Engels)—*The Economic and Philosophic Manuscripts of 1844* and *The Communist Manifesto*
- ❏ Karl Marx (with Friedrich Engels)—*The German Ideology,* including *Theses on Feuerbach* and *Introduction to the Critique of Political Economy*
- ❏ Karl Marx—*The Poverty of Philosophy*
- ❏ John Stuart Mill—*Considerations on Representative Government*
- ❏ John Stuart Mill—*On Liberty*
- ❏ John Stuart Mill—*On Socialism*
- ❏ John Stuart Mill—*The Subjection of Women*
- ❏ Montesquieu, Charles de Secondat—*The Spirit of Laws*
- ❏ Friedrich Nietzsche—*Thus Spake Zarathustra*

- ❑ Thomas Paine—*Common Sense*
- ❑ Thomas Paine—*Rights of Man*
- ❑ Plato—*Laws*
- ❑ Plato—*The Republic*
- ❑ Jean-Jacques Rousseau—*Émile*
- ❑ Jean-Jacques Rousseau—*The Social Contract*
- ❑ Mary Wollstonecraft—*A Vindication of the Rights of Men*
- ❑ Mary Wollstonecraft—*A Vindication of the Rights of Women*

GREAT MINDS PAPERBACK SERIES

ART

- ❑ Leonardo da Vinci—*A Treatise on Painting*

ECONOMICS

- ❑ Charlotte Perkins Gilman—*Women and Economics: A Study of the Economic Relation between Women and Men*
- ❑ John Maynard Keynes—*The End of Laissez Faire* and *The Economic Consequences of the Peace*
- ❑ John Maynard Keynes—*The General Theory of Employment, Interest, and Money*
- ❑ John Maynard Keynes—*A Tract on Monetary Reform*
- ❑ Thomas R. Malthus—*An Essay on the Principle of Population*
- ❑ Alfred Marshall—*Money, Credit, and Commerce*
- ❑ Alfred Marshall—*Principles of Economics*
- ❑ Karl Marx—*Theories of Surplus Value*
- ❑ John Stuart Mill—*Principles of Political Economy*
- ❑ David Ricardo—*Principles of Political Economy and Taxation*
- ❑ Adam Smith—*Wealth of Nations*
- ❑ Thorstein Veblen—*Theory of the Leisure Class*

HISTORY

- ❑ Edward Gibbon—*On Christianity*
- ❑ Alexander Hamilton, John Jay, and James Madison—*The Federalist*
- ❑ Herodotus—*The History*
- ❑ Charles Mackay—*Extraordinary Popular Delusions and the Madness of Crowds*
- ❑ Thucydides—*History of the Peloponnesian War*

LAW

- ❑ John Austin—*The Province of Jurisprudence Determined*

LITERATURE

- ❑ Jonathan Swift—*A Modest Proposal and Other Satires*
- ❑ H. G. Wells—*The Conquest of Time*

PSYCHOLOGY

☐ Sigmund Freud—*Totem and Taboo*

RELIGION/FREETHOUGHT

☐ Desiderius Erasmus—*The Praise of Folly*
☐ Thomas Henry Huxley—*Agnosticism and Christianity and Other Essays*
☐ Ernest Renan—*The Life of Jesus*
☐ Upton Sinclair—*The Profits of Religion*
☐ Elizabeth Cady Stanton—*The Woman's Bible*
☐ Voltaire—*A Treatise on Toleration and Other Essays*
☐ Andrew D. White—*A History of the Warfare of Science with Theology in Christendom*

SCIENCE

☐ Jacob Bronowski—*The Identity of Man*
☐ Nicolaus Copernicus—*On the Revolutions of Heavenly Spheres*
☐ Marie Curie—*Radioactive Substances*
☐ Charles Darwin—*The Autobiography of Charles Darwin*
☐ Charles Darwin—*The Descent of Man*
☐ Charles Darwin—*The Origin of Species*
☐ Charles Darwin—*The Voyage of the Beagle*
☐ René Descartes—*Treatise of Man*
☐ Albert Einstein—*Relativity*
☐ Michael Faraday—*The Forces of Matter*
☐ Galileo Galilei—*Dialogues Concerning Two New Sciences*
☐ Ernst Haeckel—*The Riddle of the Universe*
☐ William Harvey—*On the Motion of the Heart and Blood in Animals*
☐ Werner Heisenberg—*Physics and Philosophy*
☐ Julian Huxley—*Evolutionary Humanism*
☐ Thomas H. Huxley—*Evolution and Ethics and Science and Morals*
☐ Edward Jenner—*Vaccination against Smallpox*
☐ Johannes Kepler—*Epitome of Copernican Astronomy and Harmonies of the World*
☐ James Clerk Maxwell—*Matter and Motion*
☐ Isaac Newton—*Opticks, Or Treatise of the Reflections, Inflections, and Colours of Light*
☐ Isaac Newton—*The Principia*
☐ Louis Pasteur and Joseph Lister—*Germ Theory and Its Application to Medicine and On the Antiseptic Principle of the Practice of Surgery*
☐ William Thomson (Lord Kelvin) and Peter Guthrie Tait—*The Elements of Natural Philosophy*
☐ Alfred Russel Wallace—*Island Life*

SOCIOLOGY

☐ Emile Durkheim—*Ethics and the Sociology of Morals*